BANKRUPTCY

YOUR GUIDE TO A FRESH START

KNOWING WHAT TO EXPECT
TO AVOID THE FEAR OF THE UNKNOWN

DAVID LEWIS, JD

Cover design, interior book design,
and eBook design
by Blue Harvest Creative
www.blueharvestcreative.com

BANKRUPTCY: YOUR GUIDE TO A FRESH START

Published by
David Lewis

ISBN-13: 978-1500497118
ISBN-10: 1500497118

TABLE OF CONTENTS

This book is dedicated to the dream of a better life ahead. To finding that place of peace, security and belonging that we all seek, knowing that money alone will not get us there. I give my thanks to Mona, for always encouraging me to follow my dreams. And I give thanks to Steve Peters and Jeff McAnallen for reviewing drafts, providing comments and editorial assistance. Thanks to Gail Michael for her suggestions and editing as well. A fine wine starts with a great vinyard, but it takes a winemaker who knows how to cope with all the things that can go wrong to end up with a great wine. We all have obstacles; success comes from finding how to overcome the obstacles.

ABOUT THIS BOOK

Congratulations on taking the time to learn more about bankruptcy. This book will help you decide whether bankruptcy is right for you or not. And, if you do decide to file a bankruptcy case, it will help you understand what to watch out for, and what to expect as you go through the process of filing for bankruptcy relief.

This book is not supposed to be a guide on how to do a bankruptcy by yourself, without an attorney. It should help you decide whether you want to try that or not.

There is a lot to learn and a lot of regional differences in how bankruptcy works so it is not possible to be specific about exactly how things will work where you live, but there are some general principles that work the same way everywhere.

By reading this book you will know what questions you need to ask your attorney, and you will be less stressed by the process. If you know what to expect, the fear of the unknown can be put aside. You may get a sense of what sort of bankruptcy planning is acceptable and what is not; what types of payments you can make to creditors before you file and which you should avoid.

By using the links to jargon used in the bankruptcy world you can storm through the material like an expert and get the most out of it. There will be no test on this book and if you find yourself reading a section that does not apply to you, you can skip it. If you don't own a home, for example, you may not care to read about short-sales of a home.

This book could be much longer, everything in here could be expanded by referencing case law, competing theories, regional differences and other nuances. And if this was intended as a scholarly work it should do that. But sometimes less is more, smaller is better. For someone who just wants to know what to expect, all that detail would just confuse things. I tried to just get to the point.

As an e-book it can be revised over and over and be made better. If you see something that doesn't make sense to you, that doesn't seem consistent with what you know, write to me and let me know. Your comments will help to make this more useful to others.

introduction
BANKRUPTCY EXPLAINED

This chapter explains the entire bankruptcy process. The rest of this book just fills in the details, but there are a lot of details.

Chapter 7 bankruptcy is a process where someone who has too much debt can seek an Order from the federal bankruptcy court relieving them of that debt. The relief comes first in the form of an Order of Automatic Stay, which tells the people who are owed money, the creditors, to freeze. If all goes well, about three months later the Court enters another Order called a Discharge, which is a permanent injunction instructing the creditors to forever forget about collecting anything other than what they might collect through the Bankruptcy Court. These Orders are very powerful and will stop, at least temporarily, most creditors including mortgage holders trying to foreclose, and even the dreaded Internal Revenue Service.

Most people who file for bankruptcy relief get what they are seeking. But, as you probably know, not all debts are discharged. Some of the exceptions include student loans, child support, certain taxes (but not all taxes) and some other debts. Some debts that could be discharged are paid voluntarily after a bankruptcy. That is what often allows people to keep their home or cars. It is pretty obvious, but worth mentioning, that you cannot discharge the debt on your home or car and expect to keep that home or car without continuing to pay for them, but through the bankruptcy process you can walk away from either one without additional consequences. But, there are some unique circumstances where even those debts are adjusted.

For most people the price paid for the relief is minimal. The cost of a bankruptcy includes the unpredictable psychological impact, the direct cost in attorney's fees, and court filing fees, the indirect costs in potentially higher future borrowing costs as a result of a reduced credit score, or less access to credit and the possible loss of certain assets in a Chapter 7 case.

For Chapter 7 bankruptcy, the most common kind of bankruptcy filing, the basic tradeoff you are offering by requesting this relief is that you are willing to hand over your non-exempt assets to a trustee to be sold so that the money from that sale can reimburse your creditors for at least part of the debt. The reality in the vast majority of cases (about 94% of cases nationally) is that the things you own are considered exempt and there is no actual exchange of property for debt.

Not all bankruptcies are Chapter 7 bankruptcy. Individuals with a regular source of income might choose, or be pushed by the means-test, into filing a Chapter 13 bankruptcy. In these cases the debtors work with an attorney to develop a plan to repay creditors to the best of their ability after accounting for all the other fixed monthly expenses. These plans have to comply with various requirements to be confirmed but one of the most important things to understand is that it is NOT necessary to fully repay the creditors. They are simply paid what you can afford to pay them within 3 years or maybe 5 years and then you are done, whether the amount they recovered was 50% of the amount owed or 5% or even less. If you file for Chapter 13 relief and get a plan confirmed you generally do not need to worry about a Trustee selling off your property.

You do not need to have any minimal amount of debt to ask the court for relief, and there is no cap on the maximum amount of debt you can discharge in a Chapter 7 case.

Chapter 11 is another form of bankruptcy that often is in the news. But, for individuals it is too complicated and too expensive and almost never filed by individuals, so this book only briefly mentions that method.

 I hope I have made it sound simple, but, it is not. That's what the rest of the book is about.

SHOULD I FILE FOR BANKRUPTCY?

When I have consulted with clients about possibly filing for bankruptcy there are generally three possible outcomes. In some cases there is a combination of things that make it crystal clear that filing a bankruptcy is not a good idea. In other cases people already have their mind made up that they want to file, and I find out at the end of a consultation that the consultation was just a formality along the way. In many cases, there is not an obvious answer. In the next few sections I will discuss the alternatives to bankruptcy, the pros and cons, the various costs, and tradeoffs. These are the things that need to be considered by those people who are on the fence about filing. If you know you need to file you may want to skip ahead to those sections describing the process.

There is no mathematical formula that determines when someone can or should file bankruptcy. There is no upper limit or lower limit on the debt (in Chapter 7). There is no magical ratio of debt to income that requires a bankruptcy filing. And, although there is a procedure where creditors can literally force someone into bankruptcy, that almost never happens, and virtually all cases are filed voluntarily by people seeking escape from their creditors. Each case depends on the unique issues of that case, and each case is unique.

For those people who are uncertain whether bankruptcy is the right answer for them, I usually suggest that they go ahead and let a little more time pass, they can see whether they get the new job, the raise, the tax refund or the bonus that buys more time. If there is not a pressing need to file, like a garnishment or a foreclosure pending, and you are not sure whether it is the best thing for you to do or not, and there is something that really might happen that would help you make up your mind one way or the other, then waiting for that thing to happen is probably the best thing to do. Notice I am talking about real things not magical thinking, like winning the lottery.

However, if this goes on for months or years and many bills are delinquent, your credit rating will be destroyed, and after bankruptcy it may take longer to re-establish good credit. That's why if there is nothing specific that will change the financial course you are on, and you know that you can't make it work now, then waiting to file will not make things any better, it will just prolong the debt problems that you have. Like any major decision, it is probably best to give yourself at least a few days to think it over. This is all new to most people and taking that few days usually won't hurt anything.

chapter one

CONSIDERING BANKRUPTCY COURAGEOUSLY

There are plenty of alternatives to avoid filing bankruptcy. Most involve working more hours in the week or coming up with some cash from some other source. But when those strategies start compromising health and relationships one has to seriously question whether the avoidance of bankruptcy is worth the cost.

Often, when I consult with clients their number one question is: "Should I file for bankruptcy?" I do not answer that for people directly, but I do guide people to find their own answer, as I will here.

So, let's review all the reasons to avoid filing a bankruptcy. Go ahead, make your own list. Most people, if they are honest about it would list things like, having the boss, or the neighbors find out (**Shame**); **Fear** of the unknown; the **Cost**; the impact on their **Credit Score** (how bad is it already and what is going to prevent it from getting worse); **Pride**, or the cousin of pride, the personal values or morals that say that it is wrong to not repay a debt; and probably a bunch of answers that are based on **Misunderstandings**, misconceptions or bad information that they picked up somewhere.

When it comes to fear of the unknown or clearing up misunderstandings, this book should help you through those things. When it comes to the more personal, and emotional issues, this might help you anticipate those things. It is important to recognize that everyone feels distressed about even considering a bankruptcy filing. Virtually every person I have ever consulted about bankruptcy feels the need to apologize and explain that they didn't intend to do this, most explain that they always paid their debts; that they would continue to do so if they were able to do so. And I believe them. Nobody feels good about it. But after they have filed almost everyone feels a big relief, and almost nobody regrets the decision in hindsight.

What are some other good reasons to avoid filing a bankruptcy? If your non-exempt assets are worth a substantial percentage of the amount of your debt you are probably better off arranging your own settlements than going through bankruptcy. In other words, if you have stuff that the trustee would be allowed to take and sell, and if the money from those sales would pay a large part of the debt owed, then you might as well do it yourself as pay a Trustee to do it. But what is exempt and what is not exempt can become very complicated. If you think you would lose a lot of property and therefore you are not a good candidate for bankruptcy you may still want to discuss your situation with a bankruptcy attorney, you may find that the property you have would not be affected by a bankruptcy filing.

If your debts would not be dischargeable, or if you intend to keep property which is collateral on a secured loan, a bankruptcy filing will not help you out. For example, let's say you have a home loan ($150,000), a car loan ($9,000), a student loan ($54,000), a tax debt ($3,000) and a few credit cards ($5,000) and you want to keep the home and car. You would voluntarily continue making payments on the home and car and you would learn that neither the student loan nor the tax debt would go away. So where would that leave you? In this hypothetical example, the bankruptcy would effectively eliminate only the credit card debt. The consequences of filing would probably be greater than the benefit.

If I changed that example slightly, so that the tax debt was old enough to go away, and the credit card debt was, say, $15,000 instead of $5,000, then a bankruptcy filing may make a lot of sense.

Many people, particularly younger people, are very concerned with what a bankruptcy filing will do to their credit score. Everyone understands that there will be some price to pay by filing bankruptcy and part of that will be a likely reduction in their credit score. While that assumption is generally true, there are some cases where a bankruptcy filing could improve a credit score. If one's credit history is already blemished by car repossessions, foreclosure, or adverse judgments a bankruptcy can work like the period at the end of a sentence. It puts an end to that chapter in your life and you begin fresh from there. Future creditors do not need to be concerned about your creditors from the past coming after you and that is taken into account in establishing your credit score. The mathematical formulas used to determine credit scores are not publicly available; the companies that control these scores do not want people to learn how to manipulate their scores. However, there are instances where one can find out what effect a bankruptcy filing would have on their score. There are even web sites now that will help predict the effect on your credit score of a bankruptcy filing. I'm not sure they are worth endorsing but they do exist. The fact that a bankruptcy was filed will be reported on a credit report for at least seven years, which seems to be the convention in the industry, even though the federal law only requires such information to be purged as obsolete after ten years.

Each person's situation is unique. With assistance most people can clearly see whether or not it is right for them. It usually becomes a hard edged economic calculation about what is possible; the moral and emotional issues do not count for much when the options are limited. In other words, if your wages are being garnished or are about to be garnished, and you need everything you are making to keep your housing, and to keep your family fed and clothed, then the concerns about doing the right thing for your creditors tends to take second place to economic survival issues.

Let's review the usual fear-based reasons for avoiding bankruptcy. The number one source of fear is uncertainty. By discussing your situation with a credit counselor or bankruptcy professional, you can eliminate most of the uncertainty. You will know with relative certainty whether you might have to turn anything over to the trustee for liquidation, you will know if there are any apparent reasons why you would not be entitled to get a discharge of debt, or which debts may be excepted from discharge. You would know what the process will cost you, and you may be able to get a sense whether filing will impact your creditworthiness as much as you might think. You will probably learn or realize that your boss and your neighbors are unlikely to ever even know if you filed a bankruptcy case. Best of all, many attorneys who handle bankruptcy cases will arrange an initial consultation for free.

You may have noticed that I have approached the question from a skeptical point of view, not a positive, sales job at all. Because I am not trying to promote bankruptcy relief, I am trying to give you a realistic understanding. And part of that understanding is knowing what it can do for you as well.

So, what benefit would you get from filing for bankruptcy? First, there should be an almost immediate stop to collection calls, lawsuits, garnishments, foreclosures in process. Is that enough? By the time you are done, you should be able to get permanent protection from collection efforts directed at you personally. You should be able to get all this at a fixed and relatively low cost, the process is relatively quick, (as in done within about three months), and most of the time your only out of pocket costs will be what you pay for filing fees of $335 or so, fees of well under $50 for both the mandatory credit counseling, and budgeting certifications you must obtain from third-party providers, and attorney's fees. So, now you know why I spent nine paragraphs or so describing the negative consequences and only one describing the positive effects. The fact is that the costs to benefits ratio for most people are heavily slanted in favor of filing for bankruptcy relief.

So back to the initial question: Should I file for bankruptcy relief? You would not be reading this if you did not have some serious financial problems. You need a strategy for dealing with those problems. If one or more of the alternatives I suggested in the chapter about avoiding bankruptcy appeals to you and you think you can make it work, give it a try. If none of those seem appropriate, talk to a bankruptcy attorney. The attorney may not tell you either whether you should file or not, but after having that discussion, you may know for yourself.

This is a very generous system and it should not be abused. Unfortunately some debtors and their lawyers take on the viewpoint that if someone has decided to file for bankruptcy relief then it suddenly becomes their job to make sure that there is nothing available for their creditors. I think most people genuinely do want to repay their debts but circumstances sometimes prevent them from doing so. If they do file for relief under the bankruptcy law and have to pay something to the Trustee in the case then they are accomplishing what they want. This is not malpractice by the lawyer and it is not a tragedy. You do not have to declare war on the people who lent you money. It is not their fault. If you cannot avoid a bankruptcy filing you will know you considered the alternatives and did what had to be done. If you do file a bankruptcy case you can do it in an honorable fashion.

chapter two

ALTERNATIVES TO BANKRUPTCY

I have always counseled people that bankruptcy should be the last resort, not the first option. While the bankruptcy process has an almost magical effectiveness in wiping out debt there are consequences to filing. Probably the biggest impact of filing a bankruptcy is that your cost to borrow in the future will be higher than the cost for someone who has not filed.

For someone overwhelmed with thousands of dollars of debt, facing garnishment from their paycheck, or foreclosure of their home, the fact that an imaginary loan sometime in the future might cost more does not weigh very heavily in the decision making process.

Here's a list of alternatives; I will describe below how each one works or does not work:

- Ostrich approach—head in the sand
- Reducing Expenses
- Debt Forgiveness
- Debt Settlement Companies
- Credit Counseling Nonprofits

- Using retirement accounts
- Using home equity

OSTRICH APPROACH–HEAD IN THE SAND.

You can ignore the fact that you have a financial problem. Maybe you can ignore it a while longer. Someone doing the Ostrich plan probably stops opening their bills, and collection notices when they come in the mail. So, what happens if you simply stop paying your bills? It is usually predictable that one of the creditors will serve you with a Summons and Complaint, letting you know that you are being sued. In most places, these have to be personally delivered to you, so you'll know, even if you have stopped opening your mail. The true ostrich will ignore these papers as he ignores all unpleasant papers, and that will allow the lender to get a judgment by default. Once the debt collector has a judgment they can begin garnishing wages or levying on your bank account. Everyone knows that ignoring problems does not make them go away, but everyone wants to try it for a while. The fact that you are reading this, tells me you are tired of that approach and you know it won't work.

Although, there are some people it just might work for. If you do not have a job, nor a bank account; you have no possessions to speak of and you have no realistic prospects of earning an income due to age or disability. Those people are sometimes referred to as "judgment proof." A bankruptcy might give them some peace of mind, but their creditors are going to be unable to collect anything from them anyway, so they have nothing to protect by going bankrupt. They don't need it, and if things change for them, they can deal with it then, unless the thing that changes their life is something like an inheritance. Then they can use that money to pay their creditors. So, even for the "judgment proof" it is worth considering bankruptcy if there is some realistic expectation that you will not remain judgment proof forever.

REDUCING EXPENSES

If there is not enough money to pay the bills, many people blame themselves; it must be a result of poor planning. And, in some cases it is. But for many people, the bills were all getting paid fine until an unexpected job loss, illness or divorce happened. Many responsible people will first try to reduce expenses to make up for the loss of income. But the problem for so many is that there is not enough fat in their budgets to cut out the fat and pay just for necessities. For some, there is just not enough income and no amount of creative budgeting can make up the difference. Here's how you can tell if you are one of those people or not.

Can you avoid bankruptcy by reducing expenses? Well, maybe. Preparing a monthly budget is a good first step for anyone. And the more accurate and detailed that budget is, the more helpful it will be. For some people preparing a budget is the first time they have taken a hard look at where their money is going and they are surprised. For others, they know exactly where the money goes, there's just not enough of it.

A budget does not need to be a big deal. Here's how to do it at the simplest level. Look at take-home income first. If you're paid every two weeks you get two paychecks a month almost every month. Add those two together for monthly income. A more sophisticated budget would account for the fact that there are 30 or 31 days in a month and this method only accounts for 28 days. You can adjust for that by multiplying the sum of the two checks by 2.15, but see, already it starts sounding complicated. So forget that, just add up all the checks coming into the house every month for the income figure.

Expenses are just a little trickier. Food varies, utilities vary but some things don't. Rent or mortgage payments are generally fixed and very predictable. List all those fixed expenses that you have and add them all together and write down a total for all the fixed expenses. Don't forget expenses that happen every year but not every month, like car registration or car insurance. For these expenses put in 1/12 of the annual amount. That way you will be consistently working with monthly totals. By setting up a category of fixed expenses you simplify the addition later on when you play around with alternatives. These are constant expenses that are hard, but not impossible to change. Do <u>not</u> include any credit card payments in this category.

Then look at your bank statements, your check register, or anywhere else you have a record and add up how much you have actually spent for groceries over the last three months and divide the number by three. Do the same thing for all the money spent for fast food or restaurants, and gasoline. Make as many categories as you need, but the fewer categories you make, the simpler your budget will be. For example you could have a budget item for home heating, another for home lighting, another for water, or you could have one budget item for Utilities and put them all together. If you added twelve months of bills and divided by twelve the budget would be more accurate, because heating and cooling expenses probably fluctuate with the seasons. But we are keeping this simple so unless that is easy to do, don't bother. These expenses should then all be totaled in a category called variable expenses. Don't forget expenses that happen, but not regularly, like dental care, eye care, and new tires for the car. You may have to guess a little about the monthly average but you can get close.

Finally you have debt service. This includes credit cards, medical bills, and everything else. This is the one that will tell you exactly what the problem is and how big the problem is. Your home mortgage and your car payment are debts you are servicing but presumably you have already accounted for them. List only those payments that you have not already listed, in the amounts you customarily pay, or the minimum payments, whichever is higher. Total up your monthly obligation for debt service. Your Budget will look something like the chart below. This one does not balance. It shows greater expenses than income. It also shows that it will be virtually impossible to cut out enough of the variable expenses to avoid filing a bankruptcy case. Only a big increase in income or a sudden infusion of cash will allow things to continue. And what it does not show is how much debt needs to be repaid. The idea is to get rid of the debt and finding ways to keep paying it is only part of the answer. Those ways of repaying the debt have to be able to continue until it is all paid off or else bankruptcy will be inevitable.

In this example the budget shows that monthly expenses exceed monthly income by $605 every month. This did not come about overnight, and by shuffling things around people can be very creative and can sustain these shortfalls for a while. But it is better to understand the problem and to deal with it, because if there is this big a problem, eventually it will not be sustainable.

Another conclusion you can draw from this example is that reducing expenses will not work. They cannot be reduced enough to cover the monthly discrepancy between income and expenses. Many people are in this situation and they don't even know it. Or they make themselves sick with stress, because there is no answer they can find that will make it work. Reducing expenses for these people will not work, but bankruptcy will.

FAMILY HOUSEHOLD BUDGET EXAMPLE

INCOME		TOTALS	AVAILABLE FUNDS
BOB	$3,200		
SHIRLEY	$1,900		
	SUBTOTAL	$5,100	$5,100
FIXED EXPENSES			
RENT	$1,600		
CAR	$ 300		
STUDENT LOAN	$ 125		
INSURANCE (CAR, HEALTH & LIFE)	$ 756		
	SUBTOTAL	$2,781	$-2,781
		=	$2,319
VARIABLE EXPENSES			
GROCERIES	$ 500		
GAS & CAR MAINTENANCE	$ 320		
UTILITIES	$ 200		
CABLE/PHONE	$ 180		
MEDICAL & DENTAL	$ 50		
ALIMONY & SUPPORT	$ 400		
RECREATION	$ 60		
CHARITY	$ 10		
	SUBTOTAL	$1,720	$-1,720
		=	$ 599

FAMILY HOUSEHOLD BUDGET EXAMPLE
CONTINUED

DEBT SERVICES

VISA	$	75
CAPITAL ONE	$	60
DISCOVER	$	320
AMEX	$	49
DR. JOHNSON	$	125
LIBERTY ACQUISITIONS	$	200
ST. ANTHONY HOSPITAL	$	375

	SUBTOTAL	$1,204	$-1,204
		=	$ -605

DANGER: BUDGET DOES NOT BALANCE

If you use a spreadsheet to set up your budget you can play around with it all you want. But it is easy on a note pad too. You should have just three numbers to add up, fixed expenses, variable expenses, and debt service. Add those three numbers and subtract the result from monthly income. Is there anything left over? If there is, this exercise tells you that you can continue to manage your debt; you may even eventually pay it all off. It may be an intolerably long time before you get there but you can continue treading water for a while longer.

Can you avoid bankruptcy by belt-tightening, by reducing expenses? Go ahead; remember that the only numbers you can readily change are the variable expenses. So what if you ate more meals at home and less fast food, bought fewer clothes, drove less, how much could you save and what difference would that make. Now, think of radical change. Could you sell your car, sell your house, move into a cheaper apartment? How much would that add to your bottom line? Or, what about a second job? If making these changes is out of the question for whatever reason, and you cannot put together a realistic budget that you can live with, then you have answered a very important question about whether or not you can avoid bankruptcy by adjusting your budget.

Once there is a significant amount of credit card debt, the mathematics of working your way out of it can become very challenging. If you have $10,000 in credit card debt at an average rate of 15% interest, you would pay $1,500 per year in interest or $125 per month just for the interest. Then, if you are making minimum payments, paying 1% of the principal down with each payment, you would pay another $100 per month for that. So, by making monthly payments of $225 you could keep this going. But do you have any idea how long it would take to pay it off? The answer is that you would have to make payments for almost 28 years at that rate to pay off the debt. Are you shocked?

DEBT FORGIVENESS

Okay, so maybe you don't feel you have 28 years to pay off your debts before moving on with your life. You can't come up with more money to pay monthly. You feel the trap tightening. You know you need a break but what can you do? For one thing, you can ask for one. You can contact your creditors and ask them to forgive part of your debt. Of course, if they lose money on your account they will not want you as a customer anymore, so you have to be prepared to give up any credit account you may have. And, you really don't expect them to write the whole thing off just because you ask them to, do you? That won't happen. But, what if you could offer to pay a lump sum amount, and have them write off the difference? That might work.

Why would a credit card company be willing to do this? It's because they know what your options are, even if you don't fully understand them yet. They know that you could file for bankruptcy and get relief under the bankruptcy code. In that case they might get nothing. So they are better off settling with you for 50%, 25% or even some lower percentage of what you owe than getting nothing. So here's how it works: suppose you owe $4,000 on one of many credit cards. And suppose you can persuade that company to settle the debt for a single lump sum payment of 25% of the amount owed. You then sell property, liquidate other accounts, borrow the money from a relative or find some other way to pay the $1,000 settlement. The debt is written off, the account is closed. Nothing more is owed to that creditor. It's done. Except a few months later you might get a Form 1099 disclosing to the Internal Revenue Service that you received the equivalent of $3,000 in taxable income for "debt forgiveness."

If you settle a credit card debt for a fraction of the amount owed, the difference between what you pay and what you owed is debt that is "forgiven". That amount of debt forgiveness is theoretically taxable. You then might have to pay taxes on that "income" that you never even saw. However, this problem and this risk are way over-blown in the public imagination. If you can prove to the IRS that you were insolvent at the time, you can probably escape the tax liability. The fact that you may have tax liability as a result of debt forgiveness is no reason to avoid doing a settlement if you are aware of the potential tax consequences and have a way to deal with them. If you do not consider the tax consequences you could be trading problems with a commercial creditor for problems with the IRS. And just for clarification, this issue never comes up if someone has actually filed a bankruptcy case. In all bankruptcies the IRS understands that you are insolvent. This is a huge advantage the bankruptcy process offers over negotiating direct settlements with your creditors. It is only if you are working out your debt problems without filing for bankruptcy that you might have some explaining to do to the IRS.

If this whole concept is new to you take a minute and let this sink in. Now take that indignation you are feeling that it's unfair for the government to tax you when you did not really have any income and find a place to park it. You did get something, you bought something, or got cash, perhaps it was years ago, but you did get something for the debt you took on. You never paid taxes on the money when you got in the form of a loan, but you still got the use of whatever that you bought with that money. Now, because it is clear that you cannot afford to pay back the loan, the lender is writing it off. Is it really that unfair for the government to assert that is the same as getting free money and that free money is not necessarily tax free? Still not convinced? Fine, because as I said, most of the time nobody really has to pay taxes on this money anyway.

A bigger problem with the debt-forgiveness strategy is that there are usually many creditors and it does not really fix the problem to settle with some of them and have others that are not settled that can or will pursue payment.

If the debt problem is from a handful of small credit card bills and one or two huge hospital bills, for example, it might be better to pursue debt forgiveness. Hospitals may have foundations that help in payment, or may routinely write-off charges as uncollectable, and even if they don't if it is just one or two large debts that are causing the problem it might be best to address those directly. Much of the time, creditors do not seem to understand that they would be better off by settling either because they do not believe what they are hearing or they are institutionally unable to evaluate and judge which debts should be written off and which should be settled and which should be pursued aggressively. So the default response is to deny the request and consequently, in many instances this option does not work out adequately. In summary, settling directly with creditors sometimes works, but it is hit and miss.

DEBT SETTLEMENT BUSINESSES

Late night TV is full of commercials for companies that promise debt relief. BEWARE! Some of these may be legitimate, but many of them are predatory. One business model works like this: you agree to sign up with someone who promises to renegotiate your debts with the credit card companies. They have you sign an agreement to pay them a monthly fee. That fee is to be used for compensation for their services in negotiating with creditors, and part of the payment is to actually fund settlements with creditors. Theoretically after paying for several months the company, which generally wants to pay itself first, has a fund of several thousand dollars which can be used to settle debts. Meanwhile you have been told to skip paying on the credit cards and use your money to pay for the debt relief company. The credit card companies may or may not be aware of what's going on, but what they see is a debt that has become seriously delinquent. They probably assume that a bankruptcy filing is coming, and they realize that they would be better off getting something in a settlement rather than nothing in a bankruptcy.

Actually, we are speaking of credit card companies here. And despite what some people think, a company is not a person, and a company can never realize anything. It is more accurate to say that their computers recognize a pattern and the humans in the company have a programmed response when the computers recognize a pattern like this which is to try to negotiate a settlement. Those settlements might be for 25% of the balance or some other amount. So, if there is a $4,000 balance on a Visa card, the debt relief company might be able to negotiate a lump sum settlement of $1,000. They occasionally do exactly that, which is why they, the debt settlement companies, are not considered fraudulent criminal enterprises.

So let's imagine that the agreement with the company required monthly payments of $500. The fine print of the agreement provided that they get a fee of $2,000 for their settlement services. The debtor stops making credit card payments for six months and during that six months he has paid in to the company a total of $3,000. After six months the company has captured its fee, and settled one debt for $1,000. But nobody would do this if they only owed $4,000. There are still several thousand dollars of other credit cards that are now six months delinquent and have not been settled. Others would be willing to settle for 25% but there is no money to pay them. They file suit, start garnishing wages, and the whole settlement plan collapses.

The sad part is that anyone could do this on their own. Simply stop paying credit cards, drive their credit score into the ditch, and eventually some of the companies would come begging for settlements. There would be no fees for the service, and more money to pay settlements, but it still is not an effective strategy, because it is unpredictable and not comprehensive, and there is that potential problem with taxes as a result of debt forgiveness, mentioned above.

CREDIT COUNSELING - NONPROFITS

Beware of debt settlement businesses. There are, however, many legitimate, generally non-profit organizations, who are genuinely interested in helping people deal with their debts. These organizations also need money to operate and some of them get part of their funding from utility companies or even credit card companies. They generally do not get much from their customers. This is a trait of these companies that make them easy to spot. They may want to charge a fee of $50 or $100 to set up a new client file, which really is just a way of making sure you are serious enough about trying something and not wasting their time.

They have done a lot of settlements and they know what each creditor is willing to do. The creditors might be willing to waive interest and allow all of your payments to go toward bringing down the principal. Maybe the creditor will reduce the interest only, or require some amount that is lower than their typical minimum payment. These credit counseling agencies will develop a detailed budget, and then tell you how much you have to come up with to make a plan work. For example, they might say he needs to make a monthly payment of $500. That $500 is split up among all the creditors and there is some assurance that so long as the payments are made none of the creditors will break ranks and file suit. None will need to be calling any more either.

You will see how this is very similar to, but also very different from the payment plan that is created in a Chapter 13 Bankruptcy. In this example the credit counselor has established that the client needs to pay $500 per month. If the client cannot afford to pay that, the Plan would not start, and the credit counseling experience would not succeed. On the other hand, if that client filed for relief under Chapter 13, he could do the same sort of thing with a payment he could actually afford to pay.

The problem with the credit counseling approach for many people is that the minimum monthly payment that is needed to keep creditors away is more than they can realistically come up with. It may be a lot less than they are currently expected to pay, but it is still more than they can afford. For others, this approach works.

USING RETIREMENT ACCOUNTS OR HOME EQUITY

You may be wondering what happens to your retirement accounts if you go bankrupt. You may be thinking you would lose these anyway so you might as well use them to get out of a jam. But you are probably wrong if you are thinking this way. The reality pretty much everywhere is that there are adequate protections for the money you have saved for retirement so that it will be retained in your accounts and will not be lost to your creditors if you file for bankruptcy relief. This would be an excellent question to ask your bankruptcy attorney, "are my retirement accounts exempt?" It may depend on the type of account but most people will be assured that their accounts will not be lost if they file for bankruptcy relief.

Assuming your retirement accounts are exempt, does it make sense to tap those accounts to avoid filing a bankruptcy? The answer to that question depends on the consequences you would face for filing a bankruptcy and the consequences you would face for tapping the accounts. We have discussed some of the reasons why avoiding a bankruptcy is worth trying. But what are the consequences of tapping into retirement accounts. One consequence is that the money will not be there for you when you need it in retirement. And, given the way this money could grow tax free until retirement, it would be difficult to ever catch up with where you would have been. You will also probably have to pay taxes on the amounts you withdraw as if it were ordinary income, and if you are not old enough to withdraw the money you would have to pay a penalty of 10% for early withdrawal. So, just for example, if you wanted to get $10,000 out of a retirement account to settle a credit card debt or debts, you would have to withdraw closer to $15,000 to pay the taxes and penalties that would result from withdrawing the money.

Using retirement accounts to avoid bankruptcy is best avoided, but if you would lose other significant assets by filing bankruptcy it might work for you. Say, for example, you have $100,000 equity in your home, and your homestead exemption is much less than that. You probably would rather lose your retirement account over losing your home.

Who has equity in their homes anymore? With one-third or one-half, or whatever today's statistic is, of homeowners who are "under water," using the equity in their home is not an option because there is no equity in the home. In other words, if the loan balance of all the loans secured by your house is greater than the value of your house you have no equity, and you are "under water."

Even with the huge number of homeowners who are "under water" there are still about half or more of the homeowners who owe less on their home than the homes are worth. These people have equity. And that equity is an asset that can be pledged as collateral, which is what you do if you take out a second mortgage. In the last few years lending standards became significantly more stringent, all but eliminating second mortgages and home equity lines of credit. Before the changes that was a very popular approach to dealing with debt issues. High interest credit card debt could be consolidated into a lower interest obligation paid out over a long period of time. It didn't eliminate the debt at all but it made the monthly payments much lower and easier to bear.

Even if this option becomes widely available again, it is not a great option. You are taking unsecured debt and turning it into secured debt, for which you could end up losing your house if you are unable to continue paying.

Most states protect a great deal of home equity as a "homestead exemption" meaning that if you have equity in your home in the amount of the homestead exemption or less, that equity will all be protected for your benefit in a bankruptcy case. You would lose that protection by borrowing against the equity and pledging your home as collateral. That is why one should be very cautious about using home equity to get out of a debt problem, particularly in those cases where whatever caused the debt problem has not changed and you continue to accumulate debt.

OTHER POSSIBLE STRATEGIES

Since home values have dropped by so much in recent years, the strategies of taking out a second mortgage or selling a house to get at the equity are no longer realistic alternatives for many people. Many people wish they could sell their house but they know they owe more on it than they can expect to get from the sale. Many people have financial problems because too much of their available income is going into the cost of owning and maintaining a home that is no longer serving their needs. Some people whose financial problems can be traced back to housing costs that are too high for their income are unwilling to consider changing where they live. If you are one of those people, or even if you are not, ask yourself if you did not live where you live now, could you rent a place that would meet your needs for an amount less than you are paying for principal, interest, taxes and insurance? If the answer is yes, you may have found an answer to your cash shortfall. But to make that answer work, you would need to sell your home. Even if you owe more on it than it is worth you may be able to sell it in a Short Sale, see the section of the book that discusses short sales. That may help with cash flow, but it may not be quite as clear-cut as it looks, because if you sell your home and rent instead, you would be giving up the deductions you get on taxes for mortgage interest and property taxes you pay.

Similarly, many couples feel that they need two cars in our highly mobile society. I cannot argue when a couple says they need two cars. For many people there is just no realistic alternative. But that does not necessarily mean that someone needs two late-model, high performance cars, with high car payments. If a bankruptcy could be avoided by selling off a car and replacing it with something that is more economical to run, or cheaper to finance, that is worth considering. If you are spending as much on car payments, gas, and insurance for transportation as you are for your housing you really need to question whether there is something you could do differently.

ILLUSTRATIONS

These stories are not exactly true stories, they are based on a combination of people and true events but more than just the names have been changed. They have an element of truthiness, and, apparently, that is acceptable these days.

These are illustrations of ways people try to avoid filing bankruptcy. As you can see some of these ways work, some do not work so well.

JASON AND JESSICA – LOW INCOME, NOT GETTING BY

Jason and his girlfriend are in their early twenties. They just had a baby. Consistent work has been hard to find. But credit cards have been easy to get. When Jason files his 2013 return he reports gross income of $21,460. Jessica reports even less on her tax return. That has not been enough to keep up with their cost of living which is not extravagant in any way. When the car needs gas and there is no money in the wallet it goes on the credit card. When groceries are purchased that goes on the credit card too since it is so much easier to write one check at the end of the month rather than a check at the store each time. At Christmas, presents for the other kids in the household are also purchased with a credit card. There have been no lavish vacations, no spending sprees at the mall, nothing special at all, but over a few years the credit card balance has grown and grown and now there is over $12,000 in credit card debt outstanding.

For someone who makes $80,000 per year in household income credit card debt of $12,000 is a manageable number. For someone whose gross income is $21,460 it does not look manageable. Let's say Jason finds it overwhelming and decides to file for Chapter 7 bankruptcy. All goes well, and in a few months he is debt free. He has obtained a benefit worth $12,000, and he paid $1,000 in attorney's fees and costs to get it, for a net "gain" of $11,000.

Fast forward three years, and he has established himself in a better job that looks like it will be around a while. He and Jessica have gotten married, and they decide it's time to buy a house. They find just the right house and they apply for a mortgage on it for $150,000. Prevailing interest rates are still very low, and many borrowers qualify for a mortgage at a rate of 4.5% annual interest. Those borrowers pay a principal and interest payment of $760.03 per month and over the life of a thirty year loan they would pay $123,610.11 in total interest. But, Jason and Jessica have that troublesome bankruptcy filing to explain and they find that they can get a loan, but not at the best rate. For them the interest rate is 6%. That bumps the monthly payment up to $899.33 per month and over the life of the loan they would pay $173,757.08 in interest. That's a whopping $50,146.97 more in interest. Of course, after a few more years, if they improve their credit and if mortgage rates stay low, they could refinance the house at a lower rate and avoid paying out all that extra interest.

The point is it is good to consider the consequences including the long term consequences of a bankruptcy filing. But not everything can be solved with financial calculations. Most likely, even in this example, within a few years of starting the home loan at the higher interest rate it could be refinanced at a lower rate. The example also compares an immediate benefit of $11,000 to a long term cost of $50,000, but does not attempt to calculate the "present value" of that cost.

Along with understanding the consequences of bankruptcy it is important to understand the alternatives. This young man felt at the time that he had no choice except bankruptcy.

Well, considering some of the strategies from the previous section, was there some alternative that would have worked better?

Let's say Jason has a rich uncle. He has realized that if he had $4,000 in cash he could settle with all of his credit card companies, but he does not have $4,000 in cash. That's where the rich uncle comes in. Jason goes to his uncle, asks to borrow $4,000, and uses that to settle each of his credit cards for 25 cents on the dollar. If he is smart, and ever wants to borrow from his uncle again he repays him quickly and without ever missing a payment. That is going to be hard to do. Because the credit cards will be gone and all the current expenses will have to be paid before there is anything left for debt repayment. Everything will have to be paid at the time of purchase, and the basic problem, that the income in the household is not enough to cover the expenses still has not been fixed. So the uncle can afford to take the loss, everybody knows that, but it's harder to write off the loss of trust that results from a broken promise to repay.

So Jason decides not to even ask his uncle for a loan. He files his tax returns, and finds that he does not owe any federal income tax. He has had about $1,000 withheld from his paychecks for federal taxes over the past year, but because he qualifies for an Earned Income Credit, he finds that he is entitled to a refund of $4,500. As soon as the tax refund arrives he implements the strategy he would have done with his uncle's money and he settles all his credit card debts, on his own, and he has $500 to buy new shoes for the kids, or new tires for the car.

Implementing a strategy like this takes discipline and planning. Reality sometimes makes it impossible. The strategy could work but it is not easy.

BEN – MIDDLE INCOME, FALLEN BEHIND DUE TO UNEMPLOYMENT

Let's look at a different strategy for avoiding bankruptcy. Jason's father Ben, is not as rich as his Uncle. He has lived a very stable life, worked hard, bought a house, accumulated equity in it, but like Jason, he has used credit cards to fill in the gaps during periods of unemployment. He's making a lot more money than Jason, but he's also spending a lot more. He and his wife each make about $45,000 per year and the household income is $90,000. But they have, along with all the usual expenses, a house payment, two car payments, the boat payment, credit cards. There were also a few months of unemployment and everything has fallen behind.

Ben and his wife have built up a lot of equity in their home. After much painful discussion and searching for answers, Ben thinks he has found a way out of the dilemma. He learns that he can borrow against the equity in his house and use that money to pay off the cars and boat, and credit cards. All of that debt is at relatively high rates and together those payments were just over $2,000 per month. The new second mortgage on the house will stretch out the payments over many years, reduce the interest rate, and reduce the payment to under $900 per month, a huge monthly saving. He was on the verge of losing it all, and now it is saved and there was no bankruptcy involved. Yes, that works, but it also converts unsecured debt, or debt that could have been shed in a bankruptcy into secured debt that cannot be eliminated in a bankruptcy. Unless spending patterns change drastically, and that usually does not happen, a few years later Ben will be showing up at a bankruptcy lawyer's office with a house with no equity but two large monthly payments which will not go away following the bankruptcy, and a bunch of new credit card debt that he will be seeking to discharge.

Suppose Ben had decided to file for bankruptcy relief instead of taking out the second mortgage. Perhaps he gave up one car and the payment on it, gave up the boat and discharged the debt on the credit cards. By doing all that the $2,000 monthly expense could have been greatly reduced. The equity in the house that Ben would have used as collateral on a new loan remains unencumbered, in other words it remains Ben's property to do with as he sees fit. By filing a bankruptcy Ben could relieve himself of debt obligations and preserve his equity in his home; whereas by using the home as collateral on a home equity loan he does not actually reduce the debt at all, he just stretches out the payments and ties up the equity until the home equity line of credit is paid off.

Is that a bad idea? Well, it is a responsible approach, it allows creditors to get repaid, but it typically backfires, because the real problem comes from having debt that is too high relative to income. Typically, as soon as the monthly payments are reduced, there are new debts added and the monthly payment obligations creep back to what they were, but the amount of the debt is higher than ever, and the home equity is lower than ever.

RICK – HIGHER INCOME, SUDDEN HEALTH PROBLEM

Not all bankruptcies come about due to consistent over-spending. For some people it comes as a complete surprise, as in this illustration: Ben's other brother Rick went to work for a corporation and lives in a big city. He's worked for many years and like all of his neighbors he does not have any meaningful savings, but he feels pretty secure because he has been contributing consistently to his company's 401k Plan. He lives well but not extravagantly. He has always paid his bills on time and he has excellent credit. But last year the corporate raiders took over his company, and immediately downsized his position out of existence. He was out of work for a surprisingly long six months and eventually found a new job earning less money, but after six months he was grateful to have any decent job. During the six months he burned through the little bit of severance pay he got, and the savings he had, and relied on credit cards for the rest. It was probably related to the stress of the situation, that he had a stroke. His health had always been good and when money was tight, he let his health insurance lapse. He's almost fully recovered from the stroke. Fortunately it did not cause major damage, except to his finances. There is $60,000 of unpaid medical bills.

Rick was earning $150,000 per year, and now he's earning $100,000 per year. Most people would be envious of his income even at the lower rate. But he's got three kids, his wife does not work, and even with $100,000 per year in income there is not enough money to pay all the bills. Before the layoff the $30,000 in credit card debt felt quite manageable; after the layoff and the stroke, having $90,000 in debt between the medical bills and the credit cards feels completely overwhelming.

Rick is proud of his credit score and proud in other ways too. He has always paid his bills. He has always followed the rules. He votes Republican and he feels that we all have to be responsible for our own actions. The thought of filing bankruptcy to clear up these problems is repulsive to him. So Rick decides to tap into his 401K Plan. The Plan has accumulated $150,000 in value so there seems to be plenty there to take out $90,000 to pay off the medical bills and credit cards. He knows that he will pay taxes when he draws this money out, along with a penalty on early withdrawal. He projects that the taxes will be about 25% of the amount he takes out, and the penalty another 10%. So he'll owe taxes of $31,500 on the money he withdraws, and he has to withhold enough to cover the taxes to avoid a problem next year, so he really needs to draw out over $120,000, leaving only $30,000 in his retirement account. Rick has avoided bankruptcy but is that a good choice?

If he had left the $150,000 in his 401k account it would have been protected from his creditors. Even if he had been sued by the hospital they could not have taken that money, because it is protected. Over the years until retirement it could easily have doubled in value. He may have had the money to provide for his needs in his later years with that money. But having spent it, he has increased his chances of relying on public assistance in his later years. From what I have seen it is almost always a bad idea to tap into retirement accounts to take care of debt problems. Often, the people who do that end up filing for bankruptcy anyway and they have lost the little bit of financial security these accounts provide.

Oh, I paint a bleak picture don't I? It almost seems that there is no strategy that really works to avoid a bankruptcy and that is not true. It all depends on the nature of the debt, the amount of income, and the other available resources. A good credit counselor or attorney can help sort through the emotional issues and get to the serious financial issues and help you see what can be done.

chapter three

CHAPTER 7–THE PROCESS

OK, let's suppose you have decided that bankruptcy may be the right decision for you, what, exactly, does this involve?

I'll start with a brief description of the process.

The first step is selecting a qualified attorney to represent you and help you through this process. Later, I will discuss doing this without an attorney. It can be done, but I would not recommend it. So you should first try to find a good attorney. Many attorneys will offer a free initial consultation for bankruptcy cases. That is something you should ask about when making an appointment. Perhaps in your area of the country there is little competition among bankruptcy attorneys or a different tradition, but anytime you make an appointment you should be comfortable knowing in advance what it is going to cost you.

Think of the initial consultation as a mutual screening. You will want to decide whether you feel comfortable sharing intimate details of your life, at least details about how you spend your money, with this person. You will want to know whether they have the experience and the diligence to represent you properly. Some attorneys seem to care about how their clients will be affected, for others, it seems, they could not care less. Your general life skills should help you assess whether the person you are talking to is someone who will be doing the best they can for you, or whether you will be treated like a number.

The attorney is also screening you. Will this case have a lot of unique or unusual issues? Is this person organized or scattered? Is the household above the median in income or below it? Will you be particularly demanding, whiny, or rude? Just because you meet with an attorney and find him/her acceptable, does not mean that the attorney will want to take your case. Sometimes your case will require skills or training the attorney does not have. Perhaps the case needs to be a Chapter 13 case and the attorney only does Chapter 7 cases - yes, it does get that specialized.

Assuming you find an attorney to represent you, that attorney will need to gather a lot of financial information from you. This is usually done by means of an interview, a questionnaire, or a combination of the two. Completing this questionnaire may be the hardest part of the process for you. It does require your active involvement. You will be asked to list all of your assets and all of your debts. A qualified attorney will probably not want to take your word for it when it comes to things like the amount of your car payment. That may seem strange that the attorney wants to see your payment coupon instead of just believing you, but the attorney is responsible, as an officer of the court, for getting things right on the papers that are filed with the court, and attorneys therefore, have a duty to do some independent research to make sure that what you are saying is all correct.

People often have difficulty listing all of their debts. They may be aware of an unpaid obligation from the past, but long ago stopped getting or keeping those bills. This is nothing to lose sleep over. Often attorneys will be capable of downloading a credit report that lists all those forgotten and unpaid obligations. And while it is expected that you disclose all of your debts, in a case with no assets to distribute, even unlisted creditors may be bound by the discharge issued by the court. Even so, it is better to list debts that are disputed, contingent on something else happening, or otherwise vague, than to not list such debts.

Before you can file a bankruptcy you must get a certificate of completion of a Credit Counseling course. Using the term "course" is a bit of an overstatement. This usually consists of an hour or less of interaction with a credit counselor, on the computer, over the phone, or face to face with a counselor. I have never seen a case where someone who planned to file for bankruptcy was talked out of filing after doing their credit counseling; but I have seen people who thought they could hang on a little longer realize after doing credit counseling that bankruptcy was the only realistic option left. Congress created this requirement either because they believed that attorneys or other preparers were not adequately advising clients about all the considerations of bankruptcy filing, or simply as a way to increase the cost, and slow down the process of filing bankruptcy. They succeeded in creating one more, small hurdle to cross in order to file bankruptcy. I have never seen nor heard of anyone who went through the process of credit counseling and failed to get the certificate. But if you try to file a bankruptcy without having the proper ticket to get in, your case will be immediately thrown out. There is another ticket you need to get out of bankruptcy, which I will discuss later.

Once you have your Credit Counseling certificate and your bankruptcy filing paperwork completed you will probably meet with your attorney or a paralegal to review that paperwork and to sign it. The entire set of documents ranges from about 30 pages to 60 or more pages and could be a bit overwhelming to review. And, your review is important, because you are the person who is signing the documents *"under penalty of perjury."* A simple translation of that phrase, if you lie, you could go to jail. So it really is important that you review the documents your attorney prepared and make sure everything is in order.

Suppose you had a 2003 Dodge Ram that you traded in for a Chevy Volt, in order to cut your monthly gasoline expenses. (You are talking about changing your life, right?) OK, so that would never happen. So, let's say you traded in the Dodge Ram for a 2009 Ford F 150 after you first met with your attorney, and you mentioned that in a phone call with your attorney. But, when you review the paperwork it lists the Dodge but does not list the Ford. You may think your attorney is great and has done everything right, but if the documents do not list the Ford they are not right. Remember, you are working *with* your attorney to get things right, it is not entirely your responsibility or theirs, it is a joint effort, but you are the one who signs the papers to certify that everything is correct.

The court-appointed individuals responsible for administration of bankruptcy cases, Chapter 7 Trustees, have the ability to research public records and those records are likely to show that you own a Ford F 150, but if the bankruptcy schedules do not list it you may have a big problem. Here is a classic explanation for why something like this was not listed: "*I don't really own the truck, the bank does, I'm just making payments for it.'* That explanation is good enough to get the Trustee to demonstrate what an eye-roll looks like but may not be enough to get you out of a serious problem. Remember, ultimately you are responsible for the content of the bankruptcy documents.

The bankruptcy documents I have been referring to consist of a Voluntary Petition, a Statement of Financial Affairs, Schedules A-J, a Statement of Intentions, the means test, and various other less important documents. The Voluntary Petition includes name and address information about prior bankruptcies, and some information about the amount of debt and the value of assets which is gathered for statistical reporting purposes. The Statement of Financial Affairs has twenty questions about such things as former addresses, transfers of property, garnishments and so on. Schedules A-J includes a detailed list of property, of debts, and of income and expenses.

When you have signed-off on the bankruptcy documents and paid your fees your case is ready to be filed. Most clients picture me driving to the court house with a briefcase stuffed with papers, and handing those to a clerk to be stamped with a file stamp. Perhaps I would know this clerk and chat a bit about sports or the weather, or maybe even a little gossip about what's going on in the bankruptcy courts. Ahha, but that was the old days. Now it's a process of hitting a few buttons on the computer, entering a credit card number and the case is filed. Those of us who file regularly are not even allowed to file anything in paper form any more, and it's not because we were rude to the clerks or anything, it's just another form of progress and efficiency.

The filing of the bankruptcy case is a significant event. The world becomes divided into pre-petition (before bankruptcy) and post-petition (after bankruptcy). What happened pre-petition is of great interest to the trustee, and what is most interesting is what things looked like at that moment in time, when a snapshot was taken of your finances, at the moment of your bankruptcy filing. How much money did you have in the bank at that moment? How much money was owed to you by your employer? Were you expecting a tax refund? How long before that did you pay bills, transfer ownership, or have checks garnished? Lots of dates are calculated from the time of your bankruptcy filing going backwards and going forward. But the date of the bankruptcy filing is the one date you have complete control over. Sometimes there are strategic reasons for waiting to file or hurrying to file. Your attorney should be sensitive to these issues and file at a time when things will work out best for you.

On the back pages of the local free paper there are probably advertisements for bankruptcy professionals. These are the ones that scream - STOP GARNISHMENT! STOP FORECLOSURE! GET A FRESH START!   This is not false advertising, a bankruptcy filing can do these things. They may not disclose that they are talking about bankruptcy in the advertisement but they usually are. The way they accomplish this is that when a bankruptcy case is filed an **automatic stay** is issued by the Court and notice is sent to all creditors. This stay is automatic because it is issued in every case, immediately and without question, without the judge or a clerk even reviewing the paperwork, except in the case of a repeat filer where it is a little different. The "stay" is a temporary injunction. And, if that does not make sense just picture the IRS as a vicious dog, nipping at your legs, about to take a big bite out of you, a judge then comes along and says "Stay!" And the dog sits down and waits for the next command. Bankruptcy judges have this amazing power with the IRS, mortgage lenders, and almost everyone else. But their power does not work on some things, like criminal proceedings, child custody, support or visitation proceedings, driver's license revocation and things like that.

Another important thing to realize is that even though the automatic stay is immediate and fairly comprehensive, it does not last forever. If one of the purposes of filing a bankruptcy case is to prevent a home from being foreclosed, it might be effective, but more likely it will just slow down the foreclosure. The creditor who is trying to foreclose will file a Motion for Relief from the Automatic Stay. The relief they are seeking is an exception that will allow them to resume their efforts to foreclose. The grounds for granting that relief are specified in the Bankruptcy Code. Bankruptcy Judges might have a great deal of sympathy for someone who is in a desperate situation and is about to lose her home, but they are bound by the law. If the lender can establish that they are entitled to relief from the automatic stay under the law, they will be granted that relief, no matter how compelling the debtor's personal story is. Because of this, a foreclosure could be back on track within a month or two after a bankruptcy case is filed. The lender probably would not be so eager or able to do this in a Chapter 13 case, if there is some plan to catch up on delinquent payments.

We're talking about the process here. You have met with your attorney, assisted in the preparation of the bankruptcy documents, your case has been filed and an automatic stay has been sent to creditors. And, you know what, you're almost done. You have only two things left to do. Attend the meeting of creditors, which is also referred to as the Section 341 hearing or the First Meeting of Creditors, and file your certificate of debtor education. But the first thing you should do at that point is take a deep breath, and notice that calls from collectors have stopped. Your fresh start has already started even though you may not realize it yet, and things could still go wrong. Everything just gets quiet for about a month.

THE COST OF BANKRUPTCY

There are many costs of bankruptcy. There is a psychological cost, there is a cost to your credit rating, there is a potential to lose possessions, and there is an out of pocket cost. Evaluating and understanding these costs of bankruptcy are spread throughout this book; this section is just about the out of pocket, dollar cost of the process.

The bankruptcy court currently charges a filing fee of $335 for a Chapter 7 Bankruptcy Case. That fee can be waived under some circumstances or the court may allow payments in installments. The waiver is possible if income is less than 150% of the federal poverty line and the filer can demonstrate they are unable to pay the fee. But, if you have enough money to pay a petition preparer or pay an attorney, the court may find that you have enough money to pay the filing fee as well.

A bankruptcy petition preparer is not an attorney and is not allowed to give legal advice, even if they know from experience that people are making bad choices. Their work is limited to being a typing service, essentially typing up the information you provide on forms the court provides. The court does not require forms to be typed. People will pay from a couple hundred dollars to several hundred dollars for the services of petition preparers who remain in business by going beyond mere typing. After all, they know where to find the court and what needs to be filed. It is very rare that anyone will file a bankruptcy without some assistance.

Attorneys usually charge a fee somewhat higher than petition preparers. Since a bankruptcy client is usually not a good source of repeat business, attorneys who specialize in bankruptcy spend a lot of money on marketing their practice to constantly attract new clients. As the practice grows there is more money for more marketing, and more clients needed to pay the bills for all the advertising. And the best marketers get the most clients. That does not necessarily mean they are the best attorneys or are providing the best services to their clients. Such firms are referred to as bankruptcy mills. A bankruptcy mill may provide low cost, adequate services, but as a consumer of legal services it is helpful to shop around.

The fee for attorney's services will vary from several hundred dollars to a few thousand dollars depending on the region of the country and the complexity of the case. Most attorneys will insist on payment in full before the case is filed, for a very obvious reason. Some, however, will offer no money down plans and agree to take payment over time. The total cost of a deferred payment plan is going to be significantly higher because the attorney, like any unsecured creditor, is taking a risk that he won't be paid. The attorneys who offer such services may not be able to do so for long, because these arrangements create an inherent conflict of interest for the attorney who is trying to help a client get out of debt, except the debt owed to the attorney.

The Court Fee in a Chapter 13 case is $310, and unlike the situation in Chapter 7 cases, an attorney can recover a portion of her fees through the Plan payments if approved by the Court.

THE MEETING OF CREDITORS:

Everybody who files for bankruptcy relief has to attend a meeting of creditors. If the person filing is hospitalized, incarcerated, or serving overseas in the military at the time scheduled for the meeting, they still have to attend, although Trustees can make special arrangements to satisfy the meeting requirements. This meeting of creditors is the most visible part of the bankruptcy process and one of the most important. It causes a lot of (unnecessary) stress for a lot of people. Probably the most common reaction when a hearing is concluded is the debtor saying to his attorney: "That's it?" In other words people are usually surprised at how quick and painless the process is.

The First Meeting of Creditors is scheduled for about a month after the case is filed. It's not much of a meeting and creditors often do not participate, which may be why it is sometimes called the 341 hearing instead. Section 341 of the Bankruptcy Code describes this meeting and one of the few duties you have as a debtor is attending this meeting. Don't worry, there is not a Second or Third Meeting, but if there is a scheduling problem, or information is incomplete, the First Meeting might be continued to a later date to accommodate the scheduling conflict or to get additional information.

In most cases there are no surprises, no creditors go to the meeting, and everything goes smoothly. The Trustee calls the case, the debtors sit down at a desk at the front of a meeting room, or stand at a podium; the debtors are then sworn-in by the trustee. The Trustee's Handbook requires all trustees to ask ten specific questions. But Trustees have maintained their independence to alter the wording and the order of these questions. The mandatory questions all revolve around getting the debtor to testify under oath as to their identity, and to verify the information that was filed and submitted to the court. Occasionally a Trustee will ask someone if they listed all of their property and the debtor or the attorney will answer no, and then explain about something that was forgotten. The meeting gives debtors a chance to clean things up. The Trustee also has a chance to get explanations about things that are only briefly described in the schedules. If property was transferred, for example, asking questions about when and why it was transferred will allow the trustee to evaluate whether to try to undo the transfer or not. It is always more interesting for a trustee and more likely to lead to recoverable assets once the Trustee strays away from the mandatory questions and can get into understanding what went on that lead up to the bankruptcy.

But, the Trustee's questioning is limited by practical considerations too. In most jurisdictions the court will schedule four, five, six or more meetings of creditors every half hour. That means that a Trustee with four cases scheduled only has seven and a half minutes for any given case if he is going to remain on schedule. Some cases take less time, some take more, and often Trustee's cannot remain on schedule if there are complicated circumstances that they want to ask about and understand. Most Trustees do their best to try to remain on schedule while balancing their need to know and understand the facts in each case. This means, that the hearing in an average case will be started and finished in about five minutes. There really is no reason to stress about a hearing that will take about five minutes and you know in advance that the Trustee is looking to accomplish two things: to fulfill their statutory responsibilities and to identify assets that may be liquidated for the benefit of creditors.

This is called a meeting of creditors after all, and even though creditors don't usually bother to attend, the Trustee is required to give creditors an opportunity to ask questions as well. The time allowed to creditors can vary a great deal. A creditor may be familiar with information from a loan application and have questions like, "what happened to the stocks you listed, last year, on your loan application with a value of $50,000?" A trustee is not likely to cut-off that kind of questioning because it could lead to assets that could be recovered. On the other hand, if the creditor asking the questions is the former spouse and they are trying to get the debtor to repeat that at one time he promised to pay her parents back no matter what happens, the Trustee at some point will have to cut that questioning off. The difference in the two examples is that latter deals with broken promises and that is just what happens in bankruptcy, those promises are broken. But, if the former spouse is asking whether the debtor is trying to eliminate the debt owed to her, the meeting can be used to clarify that the debtor understands that his obligations under a child support order, or divorce decree are not being changed.

POST HEARING ISSUES:

Following the meeting of creditors the clock starts ticking out sixty days. That is the length of time creditors have for filing objections to discharge. A creditor cannot object to discharge just because they are not getting paid, or because they were promised the money, or they really need it. There are only 15 reasons why a debt may not be discharged and each of those reasons is specified in the Bankruptcy Code. It is not important for you to learn each of these reasons. Your attorney should be aware of them, and if the facts of your case could support an objection to discharge, you will probably discuss this with your attorney and have a good idea whether there is a significant risk that a creditor will try to seek an exception to your discharge, or a denial of your discharge. It is not only your creditors who might do so. The United States Trustee, an arm of the Justice Department may object, usually in those cases where their interpretation of your eligibility under the means test does not agree with your conclusion that you are eligible under the means test. In addition, the Chapter 7 Trustee may object if he/she sees a legitimate basis for objecting. Since a Chapter 7 Trustee gets no additional pay for objecting to a discharge or revoking a discharge, that type of objection will only happen in cases where it seems obvious that a debtor is trying to cheat the system or fails to cooperate with the Chapter 7 Trustee. When these objections are filed, this starts an Adversary Proceeding, which is a lawsuit, complete with exchange of information, deadlines, and a trial before the court.

If an objection is filed, the Court may still enter a discharge after the sixty days has elapsed after the meeting of creditors which give assurance to the debtor that all the debts are discharged except those specified in the Code, or those under consideration by the court in connection with a pending Adversary Proceeding.

But the court will not enter a discharge unless you can show that you have your ticket out of bankruptcy. Remember that?

Back at the beginning of the war with Iraq the Executive Branch of government was convinced that Iraq possessed Weapons of Mass Destruction, (WMD). Of course, it did not turn out to be true. About the same time there was lots of press about how bankruptcy filings were getting out of control. So in 2005 when Congress made substantial revisions to the Bankruptcy Code they bought into a line of thinking that people didn't know how to run a household budget, and that if they did, maybe bankruptcies could be prevented, or at least, repeat bankruptcies could be prevented if everybody who went through the process had to learn about how to put together a budget. The logic of this requirement was based on a faulty assumption, that bankruptcies were based on people's inability to budget. This is how government can fail, when the assumptions that were used to justify government action do not prove to be accurate, yet the policy does not change.

In my experience I have seen people's ability to budget, far exceeding Congress' ability to create a budget. The reality with bankruptcy is that it is almost always caused by something that was unforeseen or unforeseeable. People do not plan to have strokes or other disabling injuries; they don't plan to lose their jobs, get divorced, or get cancer. These are things that a budget would not typically take into account. So when these things happen people become very creative at budgeting, they hang on as long as they can, "robbing Peter to pay Paul." So it is the height of irony that Congress, which struggles annually with passing a budget - and none of these budgets balance income and expenditures, requires individuals to take a class on budgeting to get out of bankruptcy. But, such is the law. So you have to return to an agency authorized to provide debtor education courses and get another certificate. That certificate needs to be filed in your bankruptcy case before you are eligible for a discharge. There are hundreds, perhaps thousands of cases every year that are closed without a discharge being entered because someone forgot to file this certificate or didn't do so in time. If that happens there are still things that can be done to correct it, but without the discharge, creditors could then resume their efforts to collect the debt.

Alright then. We have covered the filing of the case, the meeting of creditors, and the Discharge. Is the case over? Answer is: Nearly over in most cases but nowhere close in some.

Remember that there are two things going on in a Chapter 7 bankruptcy case. First, the court is determining whether you qualify for and are entitled to get a discharge of your debts, or at least a discharge of the dischargeable debt. The second track of the bankruptcy case involves the Chapter 7 Trustee. He is trying to put some money into the hands of your creditors and earn a commission on the money that is paid out. For this second track to run its course it is not unusual for it to take months or even years. Trustees are required to administer these cases "expeditiously" and don't get paid, generally, until the money is distributed to everyone so the Trustee has no incentive to slow things down but, often it takes time to get things done. Say, for example someone is entitled to an inheritance which becomes property of the bankruptcy estate. Let's say the debtor knows that he is going to get one fifth of the money after his deceased mom's house is sold, and after the attorneys and other bills are paid in her case, the debtor estimates that will be about $20,000. Let's assume that the debts in the bankruptcy case are $60,000. You can see why he filed. The future recovery on the inheritance doesn't do any good as far as paying today's bills and even if he had the inheritance he would still be left with a lot of debt. So he gets a fresh start and gives up his right to the inheritance. The trustee, meanwhile monitors what's going on, and eventually collects the debtor's share of the inheritance. The Trustee usually cannot do much to make the probate case move any faster, and consequently it could take years to get the money into the bankruptcy estate.

It is important to understand that during this time the bankruptcy case is not "closed" even though it is likely the debtor received his discharge. This often creates confusion particularly related to selling or refinancing a house months or years after the bankruptcy. Lenders like to know that the case has been closed, but if it is not, the Trustee may be persuaded to "abandon" the house or take other action to allow the sale or refinancing to take place.

If the trustee has liquidated property or collected money he/she probably will be able to distribute some of that to creditors. Creditors are informed of this by receiving a Notice of Possible Dividend. That is one Notice that creditors should pay particular attention to. Notice that it says "possible" dividend. The trustee probably already has money or there is a very strong likelihood that the Trustee will recover money in the case, but that may not necessarily lead to a dividend for creditors. Among the reasons why not, there could be claims with higher priority than the claim of a given creditor, or maybe all of the money collected was spent on legal fees, fighting some particularly nasty battle, or maybe the money turns out to belong to a secured creditor.

When a Notice of Possible Dividend goes out, creditors have 90 days to file their claims at the Bankruptcy Court. Claims are reviewed after that. The bankruptcy estate may have to get Orders approving fees paid to lawyers hired by the estate, or accountants. A tax return may have to be filed by the estate and approved by the IRS. And even after the Chapter 7 Trustee files his/her Final Report, that is held up and reviewed by the United States Trustee, and only after they approve it is filed with the Court and creditors then have an opportunity to review it and object if appropriate. Once all such objections are resolved, or if there are none, the Final Report is approved by the Court and the Trustee distributes money according to plan. Finally after all the checks are cashed and have cleared, the Trustee prepares another report showing what happened to the money, which is reviewed again by the United States Trustee, and filed with the court. Once all of that is done, the Court staff may close the case. Given all these steps it is no wonder that bankruptcy cases take months or years to conclude if there are assets being administered.

For the individual who has filed for relief the fact that the case is open or closed is generally of no great importance. Once the discharge has been entered the debtor can usually treat the case as done. In some instances, however, if a case remains open it could create a problem with selling or refinancing a home as mentioned above.

Another common problem occurs in those cases where the trustee is able to liquidate assets or collect money and the debtor has a non-dischargeable tax obligation. Once the discharge has been entered by the Court, the IRS is free to resume its efforts to collect debts that were not discharged. The trustee may be holding money that could be used to pay off the debt to the IRS and will be used for that purpose since the IRS has a priority claim. But that promise of a future payment from the bankruptcy estate may not be sufficient to persuade the IRS to cease collection efforts and wait for payment. There is little a debtor can do to speed up the payment and sometimes the IRS is successful at extracting payment from the debtor after the bankruptcy discharge and before the money can be paid by the bankruptcy estate.

chapter four

TYPES OF BANKRUPTCY CASES

Not all bankruptcies are the same and not all are done for the same reasons. For any bankruptcy case the objective is the same, to get protection from creditors and to reorganize or discharge debt. Those who choose to file a Chapter 7 bankruptcy are required to be informed that they have other choices. It could seem overwhelming to try to learn about all the options, but as you will see, as a practical matter there are really only two options, and it is not necessary to understand all the differences in procedure. That, in fact, is what the different Chapters of the Bankruptcy Code do, they create different rules of procedure for alternative ways of getting to the same point, and that point is getting a discharge of debt.

Everybody has heard about the big corporate bankruptcies of airlines, retailers and automakers. Those cases are filed under Chapter 11 of the Bankruptcy Code. Individuals almost never file under Chapter 11. Individuals usually file for relief under Chapter 7 of the Code, but they might file for relief under Chapter 13 or in very rare instances they might file under the special provisions created for farmers and fishermen under Chapter 12. Chapter 12 looks like they took Chapter 13 and Chapter 11, photocopied it, made some minor changes and called it a separate chapter. If you like fishing and you are interested in filing a Chapter 12; forget it, unless you make at least half your income from that. There's another Chapter too, which nobody ever talked about, before Detroit filed, called Chapter 9. That's the one specially designed for municipalities. So if your town finds it is bankrupt this is the chapter they would turn to.

But for individuals or small businesses there are really only two Chapters of the Bankruptcy Code that are worth talking about. Chapter 13 is a debt repayment plan which I discuss at length in another section of this book. Chapter 7 is the most common, the quickest and the cheapest form of bankruptcy. Chapter 7 describes a liquidation procedure, but as you will see in most cases there is no actual liquidation of property involved.

CHAPTER 7 BANKRUPTCY

Chapter 7 Bankruptcy is simply a procedure authorized by 11 U.S.C. § 701 et seq. (Chapter 7 of the Federal Bankruptcy Code). Like illicit drugs that have various street names, Chapter 7 has some street names: Fresh Start, Liquidation Proceeding and Bankruptcy. Admittedly those names are not as colorful as drugs might have. The objective of filing is to get creditors off your back, for good. Lawyers would say the objective is to get a "discharge" of your debt. We're talking about the same thing just using different names for it.

At the very beginning of this book I briefly described Chapter 7 this way:

For Chapter 7 bankruptcy, the most common kind of bankruptcy filing, the basic tradeoff you are offering by requesting this relief is that you are willing to hand over your non-exempt assets to a trustee to be sold so that the money from that sale can reimburse your creditors for at least part of the debt. The reality in the vast majority of cases is that the things you own are considered exempt and there is no actual exchange of property for debt.

I'll go into a little greater detail here. When a Chapter 7 Bankruptcy is filed the Court appoints a Trustee to review the case and to conduct the meeting of creditors, from a panel of people who are trained and experienced in doing this work. That Trustee's job is first and foremost to look out for the interests of the unsecured creditors. The Trustee is not the advocate for the debtor or the representative of the debtor in the process. Many people who do not hire an attorney erroneously think they can get the trustee to help them through the process, but that is not the trustee's job. The Trustee has a role similar to a prosecutor. If he or she thinks someone is trying to break the rules the Trustee is responsible for bringing that to the attention of the United States Trustee, who is a government employee, or to the attention of the Court, which can then take steps to undo improper transactions, order the debtor to do something, or it can deny or revoke the debtor's discharge.

The Trustee may be the only person the Debtor ever deals with other than their own attorney. The Trustee reviews the paperwork filed by the debtor and conducts the meeting of creditors. Bankruptcy Judges only become involved if there is something in dispute that requires a hearing or a trial to resolve.

The Debtor, the person filing for bankruptcy relief, has only a few responsibilities. The debtor has to make sure the documents that are filed make the proper disclosures about what has gone on, what debts exist and what property is owned. The debtor has to obtain and file a certificate of credit counseling and of debtor education; the debtor has to provide the Trustee with his most recently filed tax return and has to appear personally at the meeting of creditors. That's about it.

The Trustee determines whether any property needs to be turned over or otherwise liquidated, and the Trustee eventually distributes the money received to creditors according to the priorities for distribution as established in the bankruptcy code.

The Bankruptcy Court issues a Notice of Automatic Stay when the case begins and a Notice of Discharge when the debtor has earned a discharge.

The objective for filing a Chapter 7 bankruptcy is to obtain a discharge of debt and in almost all cases the debtor does obtain a discharge. The type of debt that is discharged is quite broad, but does not include everything. Most commonly, debts for taxes, student loans, or support obligations survive a bankruptcy filing. Likewise debts for cars or homes may be discharged, but the debtor elects to keep paying those debts in order to retain the collateral (the car or the home).

Most Chapter 7 cases do not involve the actual liquidation of any property. Nationally the percentage of cases in which assets are recovered and sold is less than one in ten. In some regions of the country the percentage is higher. Much depends on what local exemptions allow, but in almost all cases you will know before the case is filed, whether it is likely or not that the Trustee will demand turnover of any money or property in your case.

When the discharge has been entered and the Trustee has completed administration of assets, if any, the person filing bankruptcy should get the benefit of a fresh start, free of most debt.

CHAPTER 13 BANKRUPTCY

Chapter 13 is all about a debt repayment plan. This is a very special kind of plan, though, because, unlike, the other systems for getting rid of debt, a Chapter 13 plan does not require you to pay off your debt. You are only required to make your best effort for a period of time, and when you have done that, your remaining debt is discharged.

This is the fundamental principle of Chapter 13, and I don't know how many times I have explained it to clients who don't understand this principal when I'm done with the explanation. So I'll say it again. Chapter 13 requires you to pay on your debts; it does not require you to pay off your debts.

In other words, it is magic. You, with the assistance of your lawyer, will devise a plan that takes into account all of your monthly necessities to be paid first, and then one monthly payment, in an amount you can afford, is paid to the Chapter 13 Trustee. The Trustee is responsible for distributing your payments to your creditors in the manner provided by the law and the Plan.

A Chapter 13 Plan typically lasts either three years (36 months) or five years (60 months). Whether the plan is proposed for three years or five years depends on what it is trying to accomplish, whether it is driven by the means test or not and other factors. Chapter 13 is not available to everybody. You do have to have an income that is predictable enough that you can plan on it. And there are limits on the amount of debt you can owe and still qualify for Chapter 13.

If someone can propose a Plan that the Court can confirm, and that plan only needs to last for three years most people would choose to end it after three years. If you were buying a car and the lender said you can pay $296 per month for this car for three years, or you can pay $296 per month for this car for five years, which would you choose?

But not everyone has that option. If you find yourself contemplating Chapter 13 because you have an income that is higher than the area median income and you don't have enough of the right kind of expenses to qualify for Chapter 7, chances are that your Chapter 13 payments will need to be paid for five years. Or maybe you are considering Chapter 13 because you have a problem with tax debt, and you have been told that debt would not be discharged in a Chapter 7 case. Maybe in your case you will try to use Chapter 13 to free yourself from your tax debt and it might take five years or so to do that.

Or, maybe you have fallen behind on your house payment. Perhaps you or your spouse were out of work, and you lived on credit cards for a while, but now you are both working again and you have to deal with a missed mortgage payment or two. But the mortgage company will not accept partial payments, they want two or three months of payments in a lump sum and you can't make that work. You realize you could pay your regular house payment plus some additional each month to catch up on those delinquent payments but they won't work with you. You cannot use Chapter 7 bankruptcy to catch up on house payments, but you can use Chapter 13 to force the lender to accept partial payments so that you can bring the mortgage current.

Chapter 13 may not be effective in reducing the amount of your house payment (although in limited circumstances it can be used to do so), and it could allow you to reduce the amount of a car payment. This touches upon something that is very much in flux, an area of the law that is unsettled and differs from one part of the country to another. I'll get back to the issues with house payments, but first, let's talk about the car payments.

Let's say you owed more on your last car than it was worth but you went out and bought a new car a couple years back, and the lender was willing to roll the existing balance due into a new loan. Your new car has lost value for a couple years, and now you owe way more to the lender than the car is worth. If you choose to do so as part of your plan you could surrender the vehicle; or what some people call a voluntary repossession. That would enable the lender to get the vehicle back which they could then sell, and they would get out of it whatever it is really worth. Since the borrower is protected by the bankruptcy filing the lender cannot get any more out of him and all they can get is what the car is worth.

Wouldn't it make sense, then, if you could keep the car and the lender could get that same amount of value out of the car? They are no worse off, and the borrower is way better off because for one thing they still have a car and they can still go to work and they can earn enough money to make payments on their Chapter 13 Plan. Once in a while, Congress is sensible, and from this comes the moderately vulgar sounding concept of "cram down."

What Chapter 13 allows borrowers to do is to estimate the value of a car, and devise a plan to pay that value, with some interest, to the lender, and cram it down their throats, whether they like it or not, forcing them to accept that value, rather than the regular car payments. For this to work the estimate of the value has to be realistic and the interest rate has to be realistic. And of course this is the kind of thing that lenders are willing to go to court to argue about, but it happens all the time.

What's really going on here, is that the system is designed to recognize the economic reality. The value of the collateral is insufficient to pay off the loan, the borrower lacks the ability to pay according to the original agreement and the system will function best if everyone recognizes that reality and moves on from there. For those who are used to following the rules, this sounds very unfair to the lender. But we make adjustments all the time in contracts. Think of what the airlines have been able to do with labor contracts in Chapter 11 cases. In those cases it became clear that the airline could not profitably operate its business with the labor costs it had agreed to pay. It would either go out of business or it would change the contracts. The bankruptcy courts in those cases forced the contracts to be changed.

So, what about a home loan, is there anything that can be done to alter the payment amount? Follow me down the rabbit hole and you'll see that the clear answer is, "maybe." Let's start with the Bankruptcy Code itself, which says in Section 506(d) "To the extent that a lien secures a claim against the debtor that is not an allowed secured claim, such lien is void, unless …" Translation - if the collateral pledged to the lender to secure the obligation is not worth what is owed, they're out of luck. That seems to mean that if you have a home loan or particularly a second mortgage and the value of the house has dropped to the point that the value of the house is less than the amount owed on the first mortgage, then the second mortgage is completely unsecured. In other words the lender thought they were getting some security by having a mortgage on your house, but if they went to foreclose their mortgage they would end up with nothing of value. They could take over your title to the house, but they would still have the obligation to the lender who holds the first mortgage to deal with. They would have to pay off the first mortgage to get clear title to the property and once they did that, they would have nothing left. Even though they did everything properly to establish their security interest, that security interest has become worthless. And once it becomes worthless, it isn't really a secured claim any more.

But, not so fast, "the law in this corner of bankruptcy practice doesn't follow such a straight path" [1] It doesn't because of a 1992 Supreme Court case known as *Dewsnup*. In that case the Supreme Court held that the bankruptcy code could not be used to modify the rights of a lender who held a security interest in the debtor's principal residence. And that remains the law of the land. But courts have found ways around that. A provision found in Chapter 13, specifically 1322(b)(2) states that a Chapter 13 Plan may: "modify the rights of holders of secured claims, *other than a claim secured only by a security interest in real property that is the debtor's principal residence, …*" And, even though this provision seems to rule-out modifying the rights of mortgage lien holders, a majority of the federal circuit courts of appeal have ruled this provision *can* be used to remove a wholly unsecured lien, even if that lien is secured against the debtor's principal residence.

Where does that leave us then? The answer is that in some circuits of the country the bankruptcy court will allow debtors in a chapter 13 case to strip-off a second mortgage if the value of the property has dropped to the point that the mortgage lender has become entirely unsecured. Or, to put it differently, one could keep their house by continuing to make payments on the first mortgage and could skip making payments on the second mortgage entirely. In other areas of the country you cannot. The answer depends on which federal

---

1   In Re: Woolsey No. 11-4014 (Dist. Of Utah, 2012).

circuit court of appeals has jurisdiction where you live. It will remain this way until this issue is brought before the United States Supreme Court and it is resolved one way or the other for the nation as a whole.

With our economy stalled by the fallout from the bursting of the housing bubble, the vast numbers of borrowers who are underwater, meaning that they owe more on their homes than those homes are worth, the large number of properties going through foreclosure it's time to recognize that the whole economy would be better off if this mess could be cleared sooner rather than later. One way of doing it would be to allow cramdown on mortgages too. After all, just as in the car example the lender who forecloses is only going to get out of the house what it is worth. But, unlike the car lender, where there may actually be a banker somewhere who holds the promissory note and lien on the car, the debt for the home loan has been sliced and diced and now may be owned by some Trust composed of a bunch of investors, and none of the individual investors is authorized to accept changes in the loans held by the investment portfolio, and the Trustee who is responsible for that portfolio is not authorized to allow changes. All they can do is what they have always done; foreclose on the property if the borrower is not making payments as agreed. Even if they would be economically better off by agreeing to accept lower payments rather than putting another house through foreclosure they literally do not have the authority to make that happen.

As I said before, Congress occasionally acts sensibly. We have a system through the Bankruptcy Courts for adjusting debt to realistic levels. This system is not fair to all concerned. Someone always gets hurt. But it is predictable, and it works. And, it is not the system that is causing the hurt, the injury has already happened, the system just forces people to face their losses and move on. This system could be adapted by a sensible Congress to help flush out the underwater mortgages and get our economy moving again. This could allow underwater borrowers to work with their mortgage companies and keep their homes. It could allow neighborhoods to remain intact. Chapter 13 is difficult, and humiliating enough that nobody should think that those who go through it are getting a free ride. They are not. They are making their best effort to deal with their debts. Perhaps a future edition of this book can skip the editorializing and just explain how a cram-down on a mortgage loan works. For now, however, it remains a muddled mess.

At this point you may be thinking that Chapter 13 might be right for you. The first question most people have is how much will I have to pay. The easy answer is: As much as you can afford. But, what does that really mean?

Finding the amount of the monthly payment is determined by the following factors:

1. Disposable income as calculated on the means test
2. Disposable income as shown on Schedules I and J
3. Best interests of creditors test
4. Requirement that all priority claims get paid in full

As you can probably tell, it can get pretty complicated to come up with the amount of the monthly payment that the plan will propose. And since this book is intended to inform you of the issues, and is not intended to substitute for the assistance you would get from an attorney I will not go into detail with all the things that go into that calculation. But I will give you a sense of where it comes from, and for many people that could be enough.

Suppose the disposable income shown on the means test is very close to the disposable income shown on the Schedules I and J. Chances are that number will be the amount of your monthly payment. Disposable income is an interesting term in the bankruptcy context. It sort of sounds like the amount of money you could afford to throw away every month, doesn't it? It is a defined term in the bankruptcy code, meaning current monthly income less amounts needed for the maintenance and support of the debtor, or amounts needed for charitable contributions up to 15% of gross income. To put it differently it is monthly income minus the usual monthly expenses, (not counting credit cards or other debt repayment). Or, for example, let's say someone brings home net pay of $2,000 monthly. And hypothetically this person has the following expenses, Rent - $900, Car payment $300, Car insurance $100, Groceries $300, Other $200. That is $1,800 in monthly expenses that will go on, regardless of whether bankruptcy is filed or not. That only leaves $200 per month to pay on the debt.

This hypothetical person also has a variety of credit cards and some old tax debt and if you were to total up just the minimum payments on these debts you might find that the creditors are expecting to get payments that are over $600 per month. That budget is not in balance. It cannot continue like that. Getting a cheaper place to rent might help a little, or working more overtime hours might close the gap some months. But, because overtime is irregular this hypothetical person is finding it hard to close the gap every month. This did not happen overnight, in fact, it has been like this for a long time. And a year or two ago there was not enough money to pay taxes and part of the debt is for income taxes of $1,871 that are still due and owing. Maybe the IRS worked out a payment plan, maybe not. But the IRS is charging a high rate of interest and that debt seems to be growing, not getting smaller. The situation seems pretty hopeless. But it is not. Not with a Chapter 13 filing.

This hypothetical debtor would propose a payment plan of $200 per month. Boom! Suddenly the IRS is off his back, calls from creditors stop, and there's enough to pay the regular monthly payments and a single check is written, or a voluntary payroll assignment is made to keep the Chapter 13 Trustee paid and eventually the plan is completed, the remaining debts are discharged.

Let's take a look at where the money goes in this case. If the Plan proposes payments of $200 per month and continues for 36 months that is a total of $7,200 that will be paid into the Plan. Possibly part of that money will be used to pay your attorney. The attorney will probably want to be paid in advance for some of the fees and costs, but may be willing to recover part of those fees from the future monthly payments. So let's say you owe your lawyer another $1,000. Once the Chapter 13 Trustee has collected enough to pay your lawyer, and if the Court has approved those fees, the Trustee pays the lawyer for you. The Trustee, of course also needs to get paid so part of the money going into the Plan will be used for that purpose. Let's say in this case that the Trustee get's 10% of the payments. The amount varies from place to place but that's reasonable. Next the trustee will take care of the priority debt. And the debt owed to the IRS is a priority, for sure. So once the money is available the IRS gets paid in full. Adding all this up so far, we have lawyer, $1,000; Trustee, $720; IRS $1,871, for a total of $3,591. Since there is only $7,200 going into the plan that leaves only $3,609 to pay all the rest of the debt.

And just for illustration let's say that the rest of the debt consists of the following Credit cards: Fingerhut $6,000; Capital One $12,000; Visa $18,000. (Yeah, I know a realistic example would include a lot more credit cards with a lot lower balances, but this is just an example). Notice how this example is set up: The credit card debt totals $36,000 but the money available to pay them only totals $3,609. That means that each creditor will get paid about 10% of the amount owed, or as people often put it, ten cents on the dollar. When the distribution is made by the Trustee, Fingerhut would get a check for $601.50; Capital One would get $1,203.60; and Visa would get $1,805.40. The amounts are not exactly ten cents on the dollar because I had that extra $9.00 to distribute. This is called a *pro rata* distribution. It means that each creditor gets paid from the pool of available funds according to the size of their claim.

So, consider what happened here. The debtor proposed a Plan in which they paid what they could afford, which turned out to be $200 per month. That Plan took care of the old tax debt completely and within three years all the other debt was taken care of too. Compare that to what would happen with say taking on a second job to come up with the $400 per month shortfall in order to keep up with the monthly minimum payments. Let's assume none of the debts are in default, and interest rates have not been jacked-up sky high. There are plenty of on-line calculators that can tell you how long it would take to pay off this debt. The one I checked, Bankrate.Com says that if you have $37,871 in debt (credit cards and taxes) and the interest rate on it is 15% it would take 125 months (over ten years), to pay that off. It the interest rate is 18% it would take 197 months with payments of $600.48 per month. Or, if the cards were in default and they put in a default rate of 29% which is not all that unusual, it would literally take an infinite amount of months to pay it off. In other words it would never be paid. The monthly payment would have to increase to well over $900 per month to be able to get it paid within ten years or so. That's a lot of overtime, or a long time at a second job.

Of course that example is probably unrealistically bleak too. By working with a credit counseling agency and establishing regular payments, it may be possible to get the creditors to ratchet back the interest rate even if it has hit 29%. And that example assumes that the creditors took advantage of the universal default clause, where if they learn that you defaulted on another credit card, they assume there is trouble brewing and they raise their interest rate to the default rate just because they are so insecure about the situation. That was a common practice before the Credit CARD Act was passed in 2009. Now that practice is banned. Instead, the card issuer can simply declare a default and demand payment of the entire balance. From the example above the actual interest rate would be a blended rate of various interest, the math would be harder to calculate, but the end result is that if the blended interest rate was much above 18% the debtor could not realistically pay off the debt with the $600 monthly payments in fewer than 20 years. Even at 18% interest it would take over 16 years to pay it off.

Compared to these alternatives, a three year plan involving payments of $200 a month must sound like magic. And it is.

chapter five

PROTECTING YOURSELF OR THOSE CLOSE TO YOU FROM A BANKRUPTCY FILING

You may think that this chapter is not for you if you are considering filing a bankruptcy case. This one is for your parents, your wife, or ex-wife, or soon to be ex-wife, your rich uncle or poor overly-generous aunt. Oh, but it's really for you too, if you care about these people and want to protect them from your bankruptcy case.

One of the most frequent issues that comes up when someone files for bankruptcy is that the Trustee wants to know if anybody got preferential treatment as you slid into bankruptcy. In other words, did you make payments to family members while nobody else was getting paid, did you transfer any property to friends, family members, business associates or did you make any unusual payments on your accounts?

The Trustee is interested in these transactions because the Trustee has the legal power to undo them, to "claw-back" the money and make it available for all of your creditors. What I am talking about are preferential transfers. These extraordinary powers that are granted to a Trustee to undo payments and transfers are very specifically defined by the Bankruptcy Code and this is not going to be a lesson on understanding what is considered a preference and what is not. It is important just to understand that if all the requirements are met, the Trustee can sue the recipient of the payment and get the money back.

In case that sounds a little too much like legalese for you, it means that if you decided to sell that 1965 Mustang Convertible you've been keeping in storage so that you could repay your sister Sally for the money she lent you, chances are that the plan will backfire and the Trustee will sue Sally and probably get a judgment against her for the amount she received in payments. This chapter is about how to avoid that kind of unpleasantness.

Believe it or not, the parts of the Bankruptcy Code that allow the Trustee to recover preferential transfers are there for your protection. If the Code did not have these provisions, the collection process would look more like a swarm of piranhas than the relatively orderly process that it is. Metaphorically speaking, if the first people to get a chunk of your flesh could swim off with it and keep it for themselves being first would pay off big time. Even second or third would pay off, so it would be a race to see who could get the most from you before you did something to stop it all. But, if everyone knows that if they get something from you and you file bankruptcy a short while later they may have to give it up, they are less likely to try to beat everyone else. It may make more sense to let some other creditor sue you and make your life unbearable so that you file, rather than being the first to take on the expense of a lawsuit.

If an individual transfers more than $600 in payment of an existing debt within 90 days before the bankruptcy filing the Trustee will want to take a look at it. But, if the person who is paid is an "insider," meaning a relative or someone close to you as the Bankruptcy Code attempts to define and then if the transfer to an insider took place *up to a year* before the bankruptcy filing, the Trustee will want to take a close look at that, because that transfer might be reversible too.

Not all transfers that happen qualify as preferential transfers. There are a bunch of exceptions, such as payments in the ordinary course. Suppose that when sister Sally lent you the money she had you sign a promissory note. And suppose you made payments at the times and in the amounts specified by the note. That would not be a preference. But, if you signed the note, told her you'd pay it when you could and didn't make any payments until the Mustang sold, that probably would be considered a preference. Facts matter.

Or suppose a young couple gets a loan from the wife's parents. (It's always the wife's parents for some reason). The money is going to be used to fix up the house so that the baby's room is done by the time the baby comes home, and some other things taken care of as well. Let's say the loan is for $50,000. The parents are making the loan to their daughter and they trust her to repay it. That trust is far more important than anything a lawyer could create, or is it?

You can hardly call the parents cheapskates, since they are willing to make an unsecured loan for$50,000. But, I know a couple of car mechanics on the radio who would call them cheapskates. They don't want to "waste" money on a lawyer. What a lawyer would feel obliged to do is to have the young couple sign a Promissory Note, and a Deed of Trust or other mortgage document. That would make everybody uncomfortable at the time but it would be far better for everyone if they had done so.

Here's how it could work. Suppose the house was purchased by the young couple for $100,000, and they made a down payment of $10,000. After getting the parent's money they paid for construction costs of $50,000 and actually increased the value of the property by that amount. The house is now worth $150,000. The liens on the house are $90,000. There is apparently $60,000 of equity in the house. Where I live, that $60,000 in equity would be exempt as part of the homestead exemption. But in many places, that equity would not be completely exempt. If you live in a place where the federal exemptions apply, the exemption protects only $21,625 of the equity. In that place the Trustee may sell the home to get the non-exempt equity out of it.

But, if the young couple had given her parents a Deed of Trust, the $50,000 loan would be secured by the property, the Trustee would have nothing to sell, the home would be kept out of the bankruptcy and the loan repaid on whatever terms the parties worked out.

Now if you are in this situation and you are thinking about filing a bankruptcy, a clever reader might decide it is time to go to a lawyer and get a Deed of Trust prepared and recorded to protect the parents. But then we circle back to the issue of preference. For it applies not only to the transfer of money but to the transfer of interests in property, such as Deeds of Trust. If you are in that fix, you might still want to get a Deed of Trust done, and then be prepared to wait at least a year before you file a bankruptcy case.

As a general rule, I would say that any attempt to give your family members preferred treatment could backfire and it is something you should discuss with your lawyer. Making sure things are done properly in the first place is the best thing you can do for those close to you. If they want documentation of a loan and some sort of security agreement it is for their protection, but it protects your ability to repay the loan too.

chapter six

MAKING A CLAIM

If you have a claim against someone who files for bankruptcy what should you do? The easy answer is there is very little you can do. Any attempt to collect the debt can subject you to sanctions from the court. But, there is one thing you need to do, if you are called upon to do it, and that is to FILE A CLAIM WITH THE COURT.

In Colorado, and probably elsewhere, when a bankruptcy case is filed a notice is sent out by the court to all the creditors in the case which says there are no assets to pay claims of creditors with. Nobody sits down and figures this out at the time, in fact nobody even looks at what was filed; that Notice just goes out in every case. As a creditor you might think that an official looking notice from the court would be correct, but it is not necessarily correct.

If you get discouraged and decide to throw away everything related to the bankruptcy case because it's an ugly reminder of what you lost, then you will also throw away the Notice of Possible Dividends that you might get. If you get that document sent to you, there is a real good chance that there has been or will be some money or property that was recovered and that creditors will get paid for the claims that they file.

It is not at all unusual for a debtor to list twenty thousand or thirty thousand in debts and none of the creditors file a claim. Imagine if the Trustee was able to recover $5,000 in the case and after expenses of administration has nearly $4,000 to distribute. If you have a claim for $6,000 you would get about 66% of the amount owed to you if nobody else files a claim. Even if everyone else filed claims and the total of the claims was $20,000, you would get a check for $1,200 (20% dividend). Filing a claim requires you to put your name and address on a claim form, list the amount owed and attach any documentation that seems relevant to showing that it is a legitimate claim. The claim form can be mailed to the bankruptcy court, or filed electronically by someone on your behalf. That's all there is to it. Months later you just might get a check in the mail. Of course you also might have a $6,000 claim in a case and you go through the bother of filing a claim and you get a check for $60.00. If it takes ten minutes to tell the court you want your share of whatever there is to distribute, how low would the amount have to be for you to say it was not worth the effort of asking for it? My guess is that it would have to be pretty low.

chapter seven

WHAT YOU GET TO KEEP IN A BANKRUPTCY

Let's just say this is a section about what property you keep and what property the bankruptcy trustee can take from you. I have mentioned elsewhere in this book that the Trustee's job in a bankruptcy case is to liquidate your non-exempt property and use the money from that to pay creditors. So the key to understanding what you keep and what you lose is knowing the difference between what's exempt and what's not exempt.

What you keep and what you lose depends on where you live.

It also depends on where you used to live if you've moved recently-meaning within the past two years.

We're talking about a federal bankruptcy law but it is applied differently all over the country. I don't want to stir up anybody's political opinions, but this is an example of how our democracy is structured, where the Federal government has limited powers, and other powers are reserved for the states or the people. There is a long historical tradition of allowing states to decide for themselves what property they will allow debtors to exempt and what property creditors can seize to satisfy a debt. The systems designed in those states generally just get imported into the bankruptcy court for purposes of determining what the Trustee can take and what the debtor gets to keep.

This stuff goes way back, and it's not all designed with bankruptcy in mind. Suppose in the old days, when things were much harsher, the local bank got a judgment against farmer John. Since John obviously did not have any money it would follow procedures to seize his farm equipment or livestock in order to satisfy the debt. But if it took everything from him, he could no longer farm or feed his family and although the bank was satisfied they would have created a burden for society. Enlightened politicians, [is that an oxymoron?], realized that it would be better to put limits on the bank so that John could keep on farming and feeding his family. So they created an exemption. They said, something like: "a debtor is entitled to exempt up to $1,000 in value for the tools, livestock or equipment used in pursuing a farming occupation." Of course they would have said it in much denser, verbose language but that would have been the gist of it. And, over the years, the amount would be adjusted from time to time, so that today the exemption might reserve $20,000 for John's farming implements.

The exemption that matters most to most people is the exemption for their cars. There seems to be a widespread belief, that a car used to get to and from work is exempt and that's that. Maybe somewhere that is true, but it's not true everywhere. Under the federal exemption, a debtor can protect $3,450 of the equity in their car, currently, and that number is adjusted all the time. In Colorado a debtor who is not elderly or disabled, can protect $5,000 of equity in one or more motor vehicles. But if the debtor is elderly, which for these purposes means over 59 years of age, or disabled, they can protect

$10,000 of their equity in their car. The extent of the exemption is different in every state. Is it for one car or more than one, does the car have to be used to get to and from work, does it apply to a motor home? The answers depend on which state you live in.

In California, the state's website, at the time of this writing says that you can exempt $2,775 of car equity, but I have it on good authority that you actually can exempt $3,525. See CCP 703.140(b)(2). But, in California, unlike Colorado, that can only be applied to one car only and cannot be split between cars.

Remember, that what I am talking about here is the equity in a car, not the value. So if you have a 2011 Ford F 150 with a blue book value of $22,000 and you have a loan on it of $17,000. You would have $5,000 equity in the truck, all of which would be exempt in Colorado. It would not be entirely exempt in California under the exemption for cars, but California, like many states has a wildcard exemption of $23,250 which is adjusted periodically. So, In California, part of the equity in the truck would be exempt under the vehicle exemption and part would be exempt under the wild card, unless that card was played to protect something else, and the Trustee would find no benefit to the bankruptcy estate in trying to liquidate that truck.

But if you have a 2004 VW Passat that is paid for, which is worth $8,450, then you have $8,450 in equity and in Colorado where you can only protect $5,000 of that equity, then the Trustee would be wanting to sell the car or find some other way to get from you the non-exempt value of $3,450.

But, if the owner of the Passat was married, and her spouse had a car he had just bought, that had no equity in it, then, at least in Colorado, the debtors could "stack" their exemptions and each claim an exemption of $5,000, thereby protecting all of the equity in the Passat.

Remember every state is different. Can you see now why nobody gives general advice about what you can exempt and what you cannot? There are huge differences depending on where you live or where you lived even two years before you filed your case.

Most places have exemptions that protect your homestead, or the value of your equity in your home, up to some fixed amount, your household goods, retirement accounts and on and on. If you are crazy enough to be trying to file a bankruptcy without an attorney it is really important to have a good understanding of the exemptions you are entitled to claim or a willingness to let go of whatever you own.

I said that the exemption for a car was the one most people were interested in, and that is true. But that is probably not the most important one. The most important exemption is for your home if you own one. These days people are not as interested in this exemption because it has become less important. With the dramatic fall in real estate values the number of people who actually have equity in their homes has declined. I recall seeing a statistic somewhere that 47% of all homeowners are "underwater" meaning they owe more on their homes than they are worth. If you are underwater on your mortgage, check out the chapter on Short Sales, you will be a lot more interested in that than the amount of your homestead exemption. Remember, the exemption only protects your equity in your home. It does not prevent your home from being foreclosed, if you cannot keep up with the payments, because when you signed the loan documents there was a clause in the fine print in which you agreed to waive your homestead exemption for the benefit of the lender.

At one time, however, the homestead exemption was a big deal. House prices were going up, everyone with some home equity felt rich. And in some parts of the country, like Texas and Florida they took that bit about your home being your castle very seriously. So seriously in fact, that they gave homeowners an unlimited exemption for their homestead equity. And it's because of these differences around the country that the exemptions that are applicable in a bankruptcy have become so complicated.

Here's why: Let's say you happen to be a former governor of the State of Texas, who got involved in some business deals that went bad and lost a lot of money. And let's say that because of these losses, you had to seek relief from creditors under the Bankruptcy Code. And, just because you were a former high flyer, the press took some interest in the bankruptcy case and noticed that you got to keep your mansion even though there was not enough money to pay your creditors and commented that, that did not seem fair. People from those states where hard working people only got to keep a fixed amount of equity in their homes noticed it too. Some of them realized that if they had some money and property, but a whole lot more debt, one thing they could do is take all their remaining money, and move to Texas or Florida and buy the biggest house that they could afford and then claim all of that equity as exempt. And for a while that worked. But that is called gaming the system, and Congress took note it was happening and as part of the bankruptcy revisions of 2005 it tried to put a stop to it.

Congress tried to stop people from gaming the system by putting in a new provision that looks at how long you have lived in your State. If you have lived where you live for less than two years, then you look at which State you lived in for six months

(180 days), right before that, and apply that state's exemptions. But much of the time the exemptions where you used to live are only available to residents of that state and obviously you don't live there anymore, so does that mean you are out of luck? No, if it looks like no state's exemptions will apply then you get to use the set of exemptions created under the federal code. And just so you know, in some states you can choose to use either the state's exemptions or the federal exemptions so that you get the best advantage. Some states have "opted out" of the federal exemptions and residents are only allowed to use the exemptions from their state.

And what has all this done? Well, undoubtedly there are now many more opportunities for gaming the system. You cannot simply move to Texas and buy a mansion right before filing for bankruptcy any more. Well, you could but that would not help protect your assets. But you may find that you get to keep your tax refund while the next guy does not, because you get to take advantage of a federal wild card exemption while another resident of the state you now live in does not get to use that exemption. It has made it much more difficult for Trustees, how can they know all the nuances of another state's exemption laws? Further complicating things for trustees is the fact that a Trustee only has 30 days to object to an exemption claimed by a debtor if it does not look appropriate. It is pretty clear that lots of lawyers make claims for exemptions for many things that are questionable, counting on the Trustee to overlook it, or not bother with an Objection. The lawyers who make outrageous or unsupported exemption claims do not get slapped for it very badly. At least not so far, but as the outrageousness increases that too is bound to change. The system only works if people are constrained from trying to game it for maximum advantage. But the game playing will go on.

If you are really insisting on trying to do your own bankruptcy without consulting with a lawyer you should try to understand which exemption law you need to apply, and what the exemptions are that you will be entitled to claim. There are two reasons for this: First, you will have some peace of mind that you will not suddenly lose some property you were expecting to keep; and second, you will not get sanctioned by the court for making an unsupported claim of exemption, when the courts do get around to sanctioning such conduct.

There are plenty of websites that are helpful in understanding exemptions. But, like anything that is found on the internet, you have to be the judge of the reliability of the information you are getting if you rely on these websites.

Bottom line - The percentage of cases where the trustee actually takes away your property and sells it for the benefit of creditors is in the single digits. That means that in 90% to 95% of all cases filed nationwide, the debtors exempt all of their property and nothing is turned over to the trustee for liquidation. But remember, where you live and how long you have lived there make all the difference. In some states the trustee's recover assets in 10% to 20% of all cases, if you live in one of those states you may be losing some property or paying something to the trustee for assets that are not exempt.

EXEMPTION SUMMARY – WHAT YOU GET TO KEEP

Cars — Equity in a car up to a specified dollar limit is exempt in most states.

Homes — Limited equity in homes occupied by the debtor is exempt in most states, some require a declaration of homestead.

Retirement Accounts — Federal law treats money in ERISA qualified accounts as not property of the estate, effectively exempting 100% of such accounts

Health Savings Accounts — Gray area, except in the 8th Circuit where a Bankruptcy Appellate Panel has held that such accounts are neither excluded as property of the estate nor exempt. See In Re: Leitch Case No. 13-6009 (8th Cir. BAP July 16, 2013).

Furniture and Personal property — Exemptions vary by state concerning what you can keep and what you cannot. Most states have fairly generous exemptions for household goods and furniture; some might mention bicycles and other states might not. Things like cameras, musical instruments, sporting goods depend on the state exemption laws are too varied to describe in any general way.

Wild Card exemptions — If the federal exemptions apply, which they do frequently for people who have lived in one state and moved to another, or for people who live in a state where either state or federal exemptions are available, the wild card allows people to exempt an additional $10,825 worth of property in addition to all the other exemptions, but only to the extent that the full value of the homestead exemption was not utilized. Some states have their own wildcard exemptions that are not tied to the homestead exemption at all and just allow debtors to lump whatever isn't otherwise exempt into this category and as long as the value does not exceed the wildcard it too is considered exempt.

Remember, this is just a brief summary; there are many other exemptions for various assets which may be applicable where you live.

chapter eight

PREBANKRUPTCY PLANNING

"Pigs get fat and Hogs get slaughtered" — unattributed

Once people begin to understand a little about the bankruptcy process and the consequences of filing Chapter 7, a light goes off in their head, and they begin to scheme about how to avoid those consequences. If an attorney tells them that they will lose their car if they file a Chapter 7 case, they might innocently ask; "What if I gave it to my wife, or my brother, or my friend?" The simple answer is, "No, bad idea."

That question shows an interest in pre-bankruptcy planning. There is nothing wrong with trying to maximize your advantages in a bankruptcy case, but there is a right way and a wrong way to do it. In the worst case you find you will not be getting a discharge, maybe you even go to jail. In the best case, you sail through the bankruptcy pleased that it did not turn out as bad as you expected. Most of the time if someone does their own pre-bankruptcy planning without proper advice, they will not end up at either of these extremes. But they may find that they have to turn something over to the trustee that they were not expecting to turn over, or that someone close has to turn something over to the trustee that was put into their hands for payment or safe keeping.

This section is not intended to guide you how to do your own pre-bankruptcy planning but it is intended to highlight some of the techniques that could be done and some of the things to watch out for. Once again, it may help you to ask your attorney the right questions.

One form of bankruptcy planning is timing the filing to make it work better. Suppose a debtor lives in a state where all or part of their income tax refund is not exempt. And, suppose that debtor files a bankruptcy case in February and then in March gets around to filing her tax returns. When she prepares the tax returns she finds she is entitled to a big refund. But, surprise, the Trustee asks a routine question at the meeting of creditors in March and learns there is a refund expected and demands that it be turned over. Delaying the filing until after the tax refund was received would have allowed that person to use the money how they wanted instead. That is pre-bankruptcy planning and there is nothing wrong with it.

CONVERTING TO EXEMPT ASSETS

The Bankruptcy Code contains a section that seems pretty clear once it is shrunk down to a readable format: The court shall grant the debtor a discharge unless…the debtor, with intent to hinder, delay, or defraud a creditor…has transferred, removed, destroyed, mutilated, or concealed…property of the debtor.[1] This language comes from another law drafted over 400 years ago in England, known as the Statute of 13 Elizabeth. In other words, one could lose their discharge by transferring their property with the intention of keeping it out of

1   See 11 U.S.C. § 727(a)(2)

the hands of their creditors. So, is transferring cash in the bank into a retirement account the kind of transfer that could cost you your right to get your debts discharged? The best answer is; "probably not." It depends on the understanding of this law that has had 400 years to evolve and be interpreted. And after going through the grinder for 400 years, you can imagine that what comes out can be pretty unrecognizable.

The number of debtors who are accused of making a fraudulent conveyance is very small, the number who are threatened with denial or revocation of their discharge as a result is smaller still. It hardly ever happens. More commonly, courts will look at transfers a debtor may have made to determine whether the property should be considered exempt or not.

Bankruptcy courts have long tolerated exemption planning the strategic transmutation of nonexempt assets into exempt assets. As stated in the legislative history to the 1978 Code: "As under current law, the debtor will be permitted to convert non-exempt property into exempt property before filing a bankruptcy petition. The practice is not fraudulent as to creditors, and permits the debtor to make full use of the exemptions to which he is entitled under the law."[2]

The Tenth Circuit has held that: "conversion of non-exempt to exempt property for the purpose of placing the property out of the reach of creditors, without more, will not deprive the debtor of the exemption to which he otherwise would be entitled."[3]

---

2   In Re: Stanton 457 R.R. 80 (Bankr. D. Nev. 2011)

3   *In re Carey*, 938 F.2d 1073, 1076 (10th Cir. 1991) (quoting *Norwest Bank Neb., N.A. v. Tveten*, 848 F.2d 871, 873-74 (8th Cir. 1988).

So what is a "strategic transmutation of nonexempt assets into exempt assets?" You might ask. It could range from buying groceries to complex retirement planning. For example, if the Trustee could take the money sitting in your bank account, but there is an exemption for something like "provisions," then stocking up on groceries before a bankruptcy transmutes your money from cash into groceries and you get to eat the groceries. If you didn't transmute the money the trustee might get it.

Once people get the idea, they probably want to strategically transmute everything they have into something that is exempt. And to a degree that is acceptable. Perhaps the camper trailer is sold and the money from it put into a retirement account. That might work. But where does this stop? Or does it?

Pre-bankruptcy planning is not without limits. Courts analyzing whether debtors have crossed the line from "pig" to "hog" look to the "badges of fraud" set forth in the Uniform Fraudulent Transfer Act and other fraudulent transfer cases.[4] A "badge of fraud" is a fact which makes a transaction suspicious, thus calling for an explanation. These so-called badges of fraud are important because they allow a court to infer what someone's intent was. That's important because it is virtually impossible to get someone to directly say that they did the transfer to keep their property out of their creditor's hands.

When it comes to pre-bankruptcy planning I don't want someone saying they got the impression that what they had in mind was OK because they read about it in this book. But I do want to provide detailed information to better inform you. The result is the unusual level of detail regarding what courts look at as described in the next couple of pages.

---

4   . In re Beaudin, No. 09-35557 EEB, 2010 WL 3748735 (Bankr. D. Colo. Sept. 21, 2010).

One Judge thought that the following questions might reveal whether the debtor had crossed the line from pig to hog and would justify denying a debtor's claim of exemption:

1. Whether the conversion was disclosed or concealed;

2. Whether the debtor was being sued or threatened with suit when the conversion was made;

3. Whether the conversion was of substantially all of the debtor's assets;

4. Whether the debtor absconded;

5. Whether the debtor removed or concealed assets;

6. Whether the debtor was insolvent or became insolvent shortly after the conversion;

7. Whether the conversion occurred shortly before or shortly after a substantial debt was incurred;

8. Whether the debtor retained control of the property transmuted;

9. The value of the asset claimed as exempt;

10. The proportion of the debtor's non-exempt assets converted into exempt form;

11. Whether the debtor borrowed funds to acquire the exempt asset;

12. Whether the debtor intended to use the exempt asset for the legislative purpose behind the claimed exemption;

13. Whether the debtor misrepresented any aspect of the transaction;

14. Whether and to what extent nonexempt assets remain available for distribution to creditors;

15. Whether the asset was a long-term holding that the debtor converted in contemplation of bankruptcy;

16. Whether the debtor's acquisition of the exempt asset deviated from his historical conduct;

17. whether the debtor sought legal advice prior to purchasing the exempt asset, and

18. The proximity in time between the act of conversion and the debtor's bankruptcy filing.

This particular list is an expansion on the criteria traditionally used to infer fraudulent intent. Section 4(a) of the Uniform Fraudulent Transfer Act contains a nonexclusive listing of the traditional badges of fraud. Section 4(b) of that act states:

In determining actual intent . . ., consideration may be given, among other factors, to whether:

- The transfer or obligation was to an insider;

- The debtor retained possession or control of the property transferred after the transfer;

- The transfer or obligation was disclosed or concealed;

- Before the transfer was made or obligation was incurred, the debtor had been sued or threatened with suit;

- The transfer was of substantially all the debtor's assets;

- The debtor absconded;

- The debtor removed or concealed assets;

- The value of the consideration received by the debtor was reasonably equivalent to the value of the asset transferred or the amount of the obligation incurred;

- The debtor was insolvent or became insolvent shortly after the transfer was made or the obligation was incurred;

- The transfer occurred shortly before or shortly after a substantial debt was incurred; and
- The debtor transferred the essential assets of the business to a lienor who transferred the assets to an insider of the debtor.[5]

Unfortunately I have had to become very technical in this section, and even resort to using footnotes. If all of that made your eyes glaze over, just remember this, there is nothing wrong with doing some pre-bankruptcy planning and it is probably advantageous to you if you do so. But, before you transfer anything it would be wise to discuss the idea with your attorney, even though that creates one of the marks of suspicion; whether you sought legal advice before purchasing the exempt asset.

To be clear, most legitimate pre-bankruptcy planning consists of either liquidating property that is not exempt and acquiring property that is exempt, or of timing the filing to coincide with a time that assets are minimized or where income is calculated lower for purposes of the means test. It is not a process of concealing assets or transferring property into different ownership. That type of planning could cost a debtor their discharge or even land them in jail.

In the next section I will discuss other reasons why you might not want to engage in a lot of sophisticated pre-bankruptcy planning.

---

5 UNIFORM FRAUDULENT TRANSFER ACT § 4(b) (1984), *reprinted in* 7A (pt. II), UNIF ORM LAWS ANN. 2 (2006) (codified in Nevada at NEV. REV. STAT. § 112.180(2)(a)-(k)).

ATTITUDE

If you wanted to repay your debts but suddenly, or not so suddenly, you found that you were unable to do so, and you found there was a way you could get out of paying them much of anything at all, would it bother you if those creditors got something from your remaining assets? Realistically, for most people, I think the answer is it would not bother them. If, for example, you were expecting a tax refund but you had to give up that refund so that it could go to your creditors. Would you resent that? There are some people who get very upset at having to give anything up as a trade-off to get a discharge of all or nearly all of their debt. But, most look at is as a pretty good bargain. If you can pay, let's say, $1,000 to the Trustee and in turn you get rid of $30,000 or $40,000 in debt, anyone should admit that is a pretty good bargain.

More importantly, there are many attorneys, probably most, who believe their obligation to their clients in a bankruptcy case is to make sure that the creditors get as little as possible. It becomes a sport of sorts, to try to make sure that assets are all exempt, and that all other legal and reasonable steps are taken to keep everything off the table so that the Trustee will have nothing to distribute to creditors.

I think for many people they are pleased to be able to see that there will be something in their case that is paid to their creditors. After all, they did not set out to hurt these people in the first place, and even if some of they have been oppressive and rude in their collection efforts, paying some token amount to them provides a psychological benefit to the debtor. But, having said that, there are frequent situations where I try to make sure that the little bit of money remaining in my client's hands stays there and does not have to be turned over to the trustee.

Timing of the filings is one of the best tools I have for doing that.

The point I am trying to make is that pre-bankruptcy planning starts with an understanding of the attitude the debtor has about paying their debts. And entering into a bankruptcy is not a reason to suddenly take on a hostile attitude toward your creditors. Attorneys seem to encourage this hostility, it's part of the persona that attorneys are supposed to have. But the best attorneys I have seen do not do this.

BUYING A CAR

Bear with me. I will focus on whether or not buying a car before filing for bankruptcy is a good idea or not, but, first, I have to give some background about this, because this is a topic that Congress really did not want you to understand. In fact Congress has written a gag rule that prevents attorneys from talking about it.

The Bankruptcy Code labels anyone who counsels people contemplating bankruptcy as "a Debt Relief Agency." This label applies to lawyers or some guy with a typewriter who is willing to take money to help prepare a bankruptcy. The Code goes on to list what such Debt relief agencies can and cannot do. In one fairly obscure section it states that a debt relief agency shall *not*:

"advise an assisted person or prospective assisted person to incur more debt in contemplation of such person filing a case under this title …"

This is really remarkable. When you look at this as simply Congress talking to some agency about what it can or cannot do, it looks like the stuff Congress does all the time. But when you stop to think that it is Congress telling lawyers what they can or cannot tell their clients in order to get the maximum benefit under the law, that's when it becomes remarkable. It is, in fact, a law intended to gag lawyers.

So why, do you think that Congress felt that it was important to include this provision in the law?

A debt relief agency means any person who provides any bankruptcy assistance to an assisted person in return for payment of money, except an author, or seller of works subject to copyright protection. Which means that by writing this book, I am exempt from the gag order, and I can tell you why they did it.

Or, at least I can tell you my opinion of why they did it. They did it because buying a car or incurring some other debt just before filing a bankruptcy could, in some cases, be a good idea. It is not a good idea in general to take on new debt just before filing bankruptcy. Most would consider that immoral, and it could end up being non-dischargeable. But taking on new debt to buy a car might be worth considering in the right circumstances.

After all, once you have filed for bankruptcy relief it's not impossible to be able to buy a car using credit, many people are surprised at the deluge of offers they get from dealers wanting to deal with debt-free customers willing to pay a very high interest rate, after they file for bankruptcy. But the interest rate you could get on a car loan will probably be much lower before you file for bankruptcy rather than after you file for bankruptcy.

Interest rates are only one reason, and probably not the most important reason to consider buying a car. The amount of a car payment is treated on the means test as a fixed expense that directly reduces the amount of money available to pay creditors. And in some cases having that expense could make the difference between passing the means test and being able to discharge debts within months in Chapter 7 versus failing the means test and being required to make payments to the Trustee for five years in a Chapter 13 case.

Whether it would make a difference in your case is impossible to know and unfortunately you cannot get candid advice from your attorney on this issue. You would be able to determine for yourself, before your case is filed, how much less money you would have available to pay creditors if you had, for example, a $400 per month car payment over the next 60 months. That would remove something less than $24,000 from the available money (since you may already be getting some credit for the car you already own). The calculation is not simple. But if you asked your attorney what effect a particular, hypothetical, car payment had on passage of the means test the attorney would probably be happy to perform the calculation for you, without comment.

If you do buy a car just before filing for bankruptcy there are other issues to be aware of. The Trustee in your case will probably check to see whether the lender properly filed its paperwork to protect its secured position. Lenders have been pretty sloppy and there have been lots of cases where the Trustee finds that you own a new car, that it is not properly secured, and that the Trustee will then want to liquidate it or settle with the lender, which could result in the loss of your new car.

If that does not happen, you will still need to consider whether or not to reaffirm the car loan. Please review the section on reaffirmation of debts because you could lose that new car if you don't do that part correctly.

So, is it a good idea to buy a new car just before filing bankruptcy? The answer is yes but only in some very specific circumstances and then, only if everything works out.

VENUE

Venue can be a big deal for lawyers, while for non-lawyers the word has a cool sound, like "Neon" but probably means nothing to them. When lawyers use the word they are talking about where you should file your bankruptcy case. For most people there is little choice involved, they file it where they live. The case is filed in the Federal District where you reside. That might be the District of Colorado, or the Southern District of New York. The location of where your hearings will be held may depend on your county of residence but you will still be in some gigantic federal district.

Where it gets interesting is when people are on the move. Moving around to be able to file in a place with better exemptions simply doesn't work anymore unless someone is very patient. If you have not lived in your current state for at least two years, then the exemptions of the place you used to live may be applied to your case even though you don't live there anymore. Or if the exemptions of that state are only available to state residents then there are some federal exemptions you may need to use.

There may be some strategic benefit in choosing to file in one place rather than another and this is one area where your attorney may not be particularly helpful. Let's say you just moved to Denver from Las Vegas. If you file your case in Denver it will be much more convenient to attend the Meeting of Creditors and any other court proceedings that may be involved. But if you filed your case in Las Vegas perhaps you would be able to use Nevada exemptions and perhaps that would be beneficial to you. Consulting with a Denver lawyer only may not be enough to determine what could have been if you filed in Vegas, and besides, that lawyer is not too likely to recommend going to someone else out of state. Fortunately, the differences in exemption laws are usually not that striking so the benefits of consulting with lawyers from each state to find which is most beneficial is usually not worth the extra effort especially after the costs of travel are factored in, but in some instances it is worth considering.

The rules about venue become important if you are pushing the envelope, trying to file your case in a place that looks like it might not be appropriate.

chapter nine

THE MEANS TEST

Back at the end of the last century there was a general belief that our computer systems would not be able to make sense of dates after 12/31/99 and that this would cause all kinds of chaos in the world. But those who partied like it was 1999 at the end of 1999 and those who didn't all woke up the next day to find that prediction did not materialize as predicted, and pretty much all of the world's computer systems went on working just the same.

At about the same time, another general alarm was that the number of bankruptcies being filed was steadily increasing, and likewise this was going to cause great chaos in the world. This rise in the number of bankruptcy filings was blamed for raising the cost of credit card interest. Your neighbors' defaults on their credit cards raised the interest you had to pay on your cards. The process, its seemed was just too easy, too subject to being abused by those who would willingly run up their credit cards to enjoy an unaffordable lifestyle, and then ditch the credit card debt in a simple bankruptcy process. Something needed to be done to stem the tide of increasing bankruptcy filings, the credit card and financial services industries pleaded.

Congress listened, and promised to do something. Of course this didn't happen right away. First there was an interesting dance, where members of Congress took campaign contributions from the bankers and industry players, promising, year after year to do something about it, but never quite having enough votes to get the job done. Eventually they were seduced into passing legislation to do what their financial backers wanted, but in an Alice in Wonderland fashion, labeling it as something else. What came out at the end of the congressional process did not even have a catchy acronym - BAPCPA, which stood for Bankruptcy Abuse Prevention, and Consumer Protection Act, and it smelled worse.

This Act had several features designed to slow down the number of bankruptcy filings. The news media got word of these changes and spread the word, the general sense came to be that bankruptcy filing was going to get much more difficult if not impossible. This lead to a giant wave of filings just before the changes in the law took effect in October of 2005.

Talk about unintended consequences, by changing the law Congress created a boom of bankruptcy filings, which were compared to a python swallowing a pig, statistically speaking. After the law took effect the filings did drop dramatically but they have been increasing ever since.

All of the hubbub was really about the creation of the means test. The idea behind it seems sound, if someone is capable of making a meaningful payment on their debts they should have to do that, rather than just walk away from the debts in a Chapter 7 proceeding. The Test was designed to be an objective way to tell whether someone could afford to pay their debts or not.

There had been a part of the bankruptcy code all along that allowed judges to dismiss a case if the judge was convinced that the case was a "substantial abuse" of the bankruptcy system. Proving that someone was abusing the system was not easy. The means test was designed to make dismissal of cases easier because at earnings levels above certain amounts a presumption was created that the filing was abusive.

And most people would agree that if people are capable of paying their debts, or some part of their debts, that is what should happen. There is a system created under Chapter 13 of the Code, which allows people to design a Plan based on what they can afford to pay, and make one monthly payment to the Chapter 13 Trustee for the length of the Plan which is typically either three years or five years. And when the Plan is completed the remainder of the debt is discharged. This system has various requirements for such a Plan to be confirmed, but paying any specific percentage of the unsecured debts is not one of those requirements. Thus, in many cases, creditors only get a small fraction of what they are owed.

The idea with the means test was to push wealthier people either out of the system or into Chapter 13 Plans. So, if you were to design a system to insure that those who could afford to do a Chapter 13 Plan would have to do that rather than Chapter 7 liquidation, how would you go about it? The devil, of course, is always in the details.

What Congress came up with was a system where the starting point is looking at median area incomes and family size. The government, of course, maintains these statistics and updates them regularly. The needs of a family of six are obviously different than the needs of a family of two. So in an attempt to be fair, they recognized that as the family size increases, the cost of basic needs would go up, and the thresholds should be different for these different family sizes. These threshold numbers, which I will call area median income, are different in different parts of the country and are different for families of different sizes. There is no single area median income number that I can refer to. This is why most attorneys will not be able to tell you right off whether you will pass the means test or not. Some of the time it is obvious that you will pass the means test and your attorney can give you that assurance without doing any detailed calculations, because if your household income is below the area median income you will pass, if it is above that, you might still pass.

When I talk about passing the means test, what I am really saying is that you can file a Chapter 7 bankruptcy case and in your filing you can check the box on the Form B22A that indicates your case should not be considered abusive. Half the people in the country can check the box with no questions asked. Half the people will have to answer more detailed questions in order to be able to check the box. (By definition, that's what median income is, half are above the number, half are below). Some will not be allowed to check the box, but they can still file a Chapter 7 bankruptcy if they think they can explain why they should be allowed to file even though the Means Test suggests that they should not be allowed relief under Chapter 7.

In addition, if the debt is primarily "non-consumer" debt you can be excused from the means test. Primarily generally means that more than half the debt is non-consumer debt. And usually applies where the debt is business debt. But in some states income tax debt is not considered consumer debt, so someone with primarily tax debt may not even have to take the means test. But just by way of caution, if you have a home mortgage, that is generally considered consumer debt and that large mortgage debt usually causes the means test to apply.

If your household income for the past six months is below the area median income you will pass the means test. You won't be interested in the detail in the rest of this chapter and can skip ahead.

If your household income is above the area median income for your family size, your case automatically becomes more interesting. A more interesting case may be good for your attorney, who may want to charge more, and it will get more attention from the United States Trustee, but it is not good for you. You may have to provide a great deal of detail to prove that you do actually qualify for Chapter 7.

Notice how I have been referring to household size. It seems a very simple question, right? For those of us growing up watching *Leave it to Beaver* if you couldn't count the number of family members you probably couldn't move on from first grade: There was the mom and dad, and Wally and the Beav. Let's see, one, two, three, and four! Apparently most members of Congress are of an age where they grew up watching *Leave it to Beaver* too.

But the world has changed since then, and the number of households that look like that are a minority now. A more realistic picture might be a household made up of a guy living with his girlfriend, she has one daughter from a previous marriage who is seventeen and lives part time in the house, and he pays child support for a son that was born to his previous girlfriend, and the son comes to live with his dad during part of the summer, or has for the last couple of years, even though that's not what the Separation Agreement says is supposed to happen. So what is that household size, two, three, four? Does it depend on when in the year the case is filed? I can't give you the answer because it depends on where you live, how the United States Trustee interprets things, how the local courts have ruled on similar cases. So much for objectivity, huh? Your attorney should be able to answer this though, that's where local knowledge comes in.

Notice, however, that I am talking about household income. Let's look at the example of the guy living with his girlfriend in an established household. This couple is not married, and even though they may have used credit for mutual purposes they cannot file a bankruptcy case as a couple, unless they qualify as a couple that is married under common law. But even though they are not married, and even though all the debts are in the guy's name, (in this hypothetical situation), the girlfriend's income still may count in determining whether or not the guy can qualify for Chapter 7 bankruptcy if she is sharing in paying the household expenses.

In my opinion, this is one of the biggest, sneakiest changes the so-called reform of the bankruptcy law brought about. Did you ever consider that your boyfriend or girlfriend, husband or wife, is now legally obligated to back you up on repayment of your debts? They may have had nothing to do with the creation of those debts; they may not have even been around at the time. In some states spouses have had some legal responsibility for their spouse's debts all along, but, that is not the case in all states. Many have allowed each spouse to be individually responsible for their debt. This change in the bankruptcy law shifts that. If your spouse (or significant other) is making money and they are part of the household, their earnings may count toward the total household income, and because of their earnings, you may not qualify for Chapter 7. They may not be required to actually pay your debts, but their income may limit your bank-ruptcy options.

Consider the implications. Let's say your crazy husband de-cides it is time to quit his job and go work on the invention he is passionate about. You, on the other hand, are the rational one, keeping your job with the school district while he tinkers for months in the garage. He taps into his credit cards, takes out a home equity line of credit, gets a patent, but eventually finds that the world is not ready for his invention, or that he will need to raise two million dollars to do a proper marketing campaign and there are no investors willing to put their money in. His credit cards are maxed out, there is no money to live on, and he goes back to work for an established engineering firm at a good salary. Now he has a good job, but there are hundreds of thousands of dollars of debt, even with a good salary and your income, there is no way to keep up with all the debt. He gets sued. Then he gets garnished. And without his full income you can't make the house payment and suddenly it looks like you, your reformed husband, and kids will be out on the street soon unless bankruptcy can help you out.

Remember, you were very careful not to use your credit to fund this; you did not incur any debt. But now, suddenly you find that with his income and yours your family's income is too high to qualify for Chapter 7 and your family will have to spend the next five years repaying the debt he ran up. Is that fair? Some would say yes, some would say no. But whether you agree or disagree with the fairness, you are a guaran-tor of the debt of members of your household, whether you knew it or not. Your income is part of the household income that is used to calculate what his payments will need to be if he files a Chapter 13 case.

Or, maybe not. In this example, it might depend on how the borrowed money was used. Did he borrow against his credit cards to pay living expenses, or did he borrow to pay business expenses? If the debt is primarily business debt, you can skip the means test. But there is one big problem. If you have a home mortgage that is considered consumer debt. So, even if tens of thousands of debt was created in attempting to start a business that did not succeed, if you have a home, and a home mortgage chances are that your debt will be considered primarily consumer debt and you will be subject to the means test. Tax debt, on the other hand is not considered consumer debt. Go figure.

As a lawyer I have found it difficult to explain to clients why I need to see their spouse's paystubs in those cases where the spouse does not plan to participate in the bankruptcy filing. Not only do I need to see them, I have to file them with the court.

If something so seemingly simple as household size becomes that difficult, you can imagine the possibilities for the other issues created by the means test.

One thing that is very important to understand if you are trying to understand the means test is that it is not based on reality, it is not intended to reflect reality, it is a fiction of the way things could be. In a bankruptcy filing Schedule I shows your current or projected income, and Schedule J shows your current or projected expenses. Since these are supposed to be projections there is often some fiction in these too, but they are closer to reality. For example, you are being foreclosed out of your house and you know you will have to rent a place. You think you can find a place for about $1,000 a month. You're not paying that now, and don't really know when it will start. That's a fiction, but it is a good faith estimate of what you expect things to look like. The means test on the other hand is a pure fiction.

You probably have monthly payments that are more than your monthly income or you would not be considering bankruptcy. But the means test is not concerned with reality. It is more of a test of whether, if you lived closer to some statistical model, you would have enough money to pay for necessities and some left over to pay creditors.

And guess where this statistical model came from? IRS collection standards, that's where. That's right, after collecting from deadbeat taxpayers for years, the Service developed certain standards for how much they thought was adequate for people to spend on food, toothpaste, cars and transportation, housing, everything else. If someone took home $2,000 a month and lived in a particular county, the Service would set the amount they needed to pay to repay delinquent taxes by factoring in these collection standards. So essentially Congress determined that if those standards were good enough for the IRS they should be good enough for all the private sector creditors out there too.

The way this works, then, is that as of 2011 if someone lived in Boulder County, Colorado and has a household size of two, the means test would allow $60 per person per month for health care expenses (for those under 65); it would allow $1,072 for mortgage payment or rent expense; $236 for the expense of operating one car, a little less for the second car if there are two in the household, and actual amounts for various other things like health insurance, charitable contributions, certain parts of the phone bill - but not the whole thing.

While the actual allowances vary from place to place and get revised regularly, the important thing to understand is that most people do not spend exactly $1,072 for their cost of housing or $236 monthly for the gas, oil changes, registration and maintenance to keep their car on the road. Someone with a long commute probably spends a lot more than that monthly but the means test will not allow an actual cost to be listed on the form. It is, after all a fiction. The fiction being that if you did spend no more than $236 on such expenses you might end up with some money to pay your creditors, so we, (Congress) are going to assume that if you do not have that extra money to pay your creditors your filing under Chapter 7 is an abuse of the system. Another way of looking at this is that if a client said they actually spent $400 a month for gasoline because they went skiing every weekend, you can see why there is some logic in just picking a number and saying its reasonable, rather than arguing about whether the guy should be going skiing or not.

I have made this means test sound very onerous and for some people it is. But the surprising thing is that there are some people with very high income that still can pass the test. How is that possible? The answer lies in having real expenses that the means test allows you to take full advantage of.

I have talked about allowances and actual expenses, but I haven't explained the big picture yet. Here's how it works: You begin with your household income over the past six months. If you were out of work for part of that time it helps to bring down your average monthly income, if you got a bonus during that time it tends to push it up. The six month income is doubled to see what it would look like on an annual basis. That number is compared with the area median income for your size household. If your number is below the median, you pass, end of test. If your number is above the area median, you have to engage in the fiction of the rest of the test. Let's say, for example that you have a first and second mortgage, you are current on both and you hope to be able to keep your house. And just for this example, let's say that the total of the first and second mortgage payments is $2,685.42 per month. Remember I said that in Boulder County there was a housing allowance of $1,072, and all that stuff about fiction and reality. Here is where reality is allowed back in. Since the mortgage payments are greater than the housing allowance they are subtracted from the allowance and you are allowed nothing for a housing allowance. However, you are allowed to claim as a deduction against your income, the $2,685.42 that you are actually paying to the secured creditors that hold the mortgage on your house. Those payments, by themselves, without even getting into other deductions or allowances may be enough to allow you to pass the means test. Essentially you add up all the fictional allowances you are permitted along with only the actual expenses that are allowed and subtract that number from your income to show how much you have available, theoretically, to pay your creditors. The final phase of the means test looks at whether that theoretical payment would be enough to make any real difference to your creditors. Suppose after doing all the math I just described the answer was that you had just enough to pay $100 a year to your creditors; is that enough to make a difference? The answer is no.

What the law actually says is, and don't worry, you don't need to learn this, it's really just an example of how this gets complicated: If the debtor's current monthly income [minus stuff as described above] multiplied by 60 is not less than the lesser of 25% of the ...claims, or $7,025, whichever is greater, or $11,725. In other words if your theoretical disposable income would be enough to pay 25 cents on the dollar for each of your debts or at least $7,025 or if that multiplied number works out to more than $11,725. Then you have enough to pay your creditors and cannot file a Chapter 7 case without proving some special circumstances. Five times twelve is 60, that's where the 60 comes from, because Congress was looking at how much could be repaid in five years. $11,725 divided by 60 equals $195.41. The engineers and mathematicians reading this might appreciate the detail, for everyone else, the computer will tell you.

So if you have discretionary income of around $200 per month you may not be able to pass the means test. But don't despair. You are probably thinking that you do have discretionary income of $200 per month or more and that you may not be able to pass the means test. How do you know? Well you know that somehow you have been making payments on credit card debt of several hundred dollars a month and kept up on all the other payments too. You might reach the conclusion that you will have a problem with the means test. But this is where a little knowledge is a dangerous thing. You probably don't know how your spending and the imaginary world of the means test compare. It is really only by crunching the numbers that anyone will know.

And here is something that Congress does not want you to know. Remember how the payments to secured creditors are allowed as deductions for the full amounts of those payments? Suppose there are two debtors who both live in the same community, both have the same size family, both work at the same employer and earn the same amount of money, in fact they both took out mortgages on their homes in exactly the same amount. They are financially speaking, twins. The only difference between these two is that one of them has a car payment and the other does not. Does the responsible one who realized he could not afford a new car get rewarded for his good sense? No, it is just the opposite. In this example it would be possible that one of these debtors would fail to pass the means test and the other one, the one who bought the new car, would pass the means test. That means the one with the new car gets the benefit of driving around in a new car while his twin spends the next five years repaying creditors. Perhaps, like much of what has come out of Congress recently, the Bankruptcy law was intended to help certain business interests, as much as it was intended to encourage responsible behavior.

So why do I say that Congress does not want you to know about how this works. I think this provision of the law explains why I say that. Section 526 specifically prohibits those who assist people in filing for bankruptcy from doing several things including *advise an assisted person for prospective assisted person to incur more debt in contemplation of such person filing a case under this title...* In other words your attorney is barred from telling you that although you can't pass the means test now, maybe if you went out and bought a new car and had car payments then you could pass the means test.

Am I suggesting that you go out and do that, certainly not. Whether you need it, can afford it, and whether it would make any difference at all in your individual circumstances I cannot say. Unfortunately neither can your attorney; they have been gagged by this provision of the law. If you did want to buy a new car before you filed for bankruptcy, knowing that your car is on its last legs, and perhaps you still have relatively good credit and you are expecting it will be more difficult to buy one afterwards, then your attorney probably could calculate whether your idea would make any difference in whether or not you pass the means test.

BUSINESS DEBT – **AN EXCEPTION TO THE MEANS TEST**

A person whose debts are primarily business debt can claim an exception to the means testing formula and get relief under chapter 7 even with a high income. The key, however, is showing that debts are primarily business debts. That can get tricky in a couple of ways. For one, people often use personal credit cards for business purposes, or mixed even, for both business and personal purposes. So if the MasterCard has a $10,000 balance that was accumulated for both business and personal reasons some portion may be business debt and some portion may not.

A bigger factor for most people is their home mortgage. A home mortgage is considered a personal debt. So, even if you were engaged in business and ran up $300,000 in debt related to the business, if you have a home mortgage and you owe $301,000 on it, your debts would not be considered primarily business debts.

Interestingly, debt owed to the IRS does not add to your personal debt obligation for these purposes. Ultimately, to be excepted from means testing because the debt is primarily business debt you will need to divide up the business debt and the personal debt and see which is the higher total. If there is more business debt than personal debt, you may be excepted from the means test.

You might have concluded that I have a bit if a cynical attitude about the means test and yes, I do. From my personal experience I would still say that most people genuinely do want to pay back their debts. For some it becomes impossible. To be facing that situation and then have someone telling you that you make too much money to be able to file for Chapter 7 even though you lost your job two months ago and have no prospects for employment, it is enough to make one cynical. I don't think there ever was a crisis in abusive bankruptcy filings, at least not in the area where I worked. This crisis was another manufactured crisis, much like the elusive weapons of mass destruction that were never found in Iraq.

So, although I am a little cynical about this means test, it is the law, it is important to understand it, and if you do not pass the means test that does not mean that you cannot file for bankruptcy relief. You just cannot file a Chapter 7 bankruptcy case. In fact, you might have enough income that you could restructure your debt in a Chapter 13 case and deal very effectively with it that way.

chapter ten

KEEPING THE CAR: REAFIRMATION AGREEMENTS

If you own a car, truck, motorcycle, or a boat, or a recreational vehicle or even a washing machine that you are making payments on you probably do need to read and understand this chapter. If you don't have any secured debts of this kind you can skip it. But wait until after the next paragraph to make sure.

Notice I did not include a home loan in the secured debts I described. If you have a home loan and you file for bankruptcy it is likely that the lender will ask you to reaffirm the debt. You do not have to sign a reaffirmation agreement in order to keep your house and usually it is not a good idea to do that. If you want to understand why, read on.

A reaffirmation agreement is a written agreement that follows a particular kind of form, which is intended to be filed with the Court and approved by a Judge. You are Affirming all over again that you will agree to pay the loan according to the terms of the agreement, you are Re-affirming. If you do all the steps properly and the agreement is approved by the court, the lender basically has the right to treat the loan as if there never was a bankruptcy involved. Typically the loan gets repaid and everybody's happy. But if things go from bad to worse, and following a bankruptcy you default on a reaffirmed debt, the lender has all their usual remedies, as if no bankruptcy was ever filed, you could be sued, wages garnished and so on.

You can see why lenders like these agreements, but for debtors they are something to avoid, if possible. When it comes to a home loan, the lender will probably offer to put the loan back on an automatic payment status, or they might say they cannot send you monthly statements unless you reaffirm the debt. In some cases they might report to a credit bureau that the loan was discharged by a bankruptcy, which is technically true, even if you have been making consistent monthly payments following the bankruptcy. Such tactics are just tactics. They can be inconvenient or harmful, but they are not the kind of thing that could result in the loss of your house. Just because you went bankrupt does not mean that you defaulted on your home loan, and your agreement with your mortgagor basically says they can only foreclose on your home if you default on the agreement. Even if the agreement says that filing for bankruptcy is a default, that provision of the agreement is not legally enforceable, they cannot foreclose your home just because of a bankruptcy filing. But they can foreclose if you don't make the payments consistently according to the loan terms.

For a long time car loans worked much the same way, but then the law changed. After the law changed, you have to decide on one of four options: 1) surrender the car; 2) reaffirm the car loan; 3) redeem from the lender or 4) play chicken with the lender by keeping the car, keeping up payments and hoping they don't decide to repossess the car. For most people this is a very tough decision. You will announce your decision about how you expect to treat your secured loans with your original bankruptcy filing, but you are simply indicating your intention, and those intentions could change. You are supposed to follow through on these intentions quickly after filing, but those rules are not enforced diligently.

For some people who are badly underwater on their car loans, owing a vast amount more than the car is worth, it should not be a tough decision at all. The debtor should simply turn the car back in and forget about the debt.

What if you have a minivan worth $6,000 and you owe $7,000? And, let's say you are happy with it, it works well for you, you're pretty sure you can afford the car payments. You also realize that shopping for a new car is a hassle, that you've got nothing for a down payment, and re-doing registration and all that, and you know that after filing for bankruptcy you will be paying a higher than normal interest rate on a car loan. Once all of that is factored in, it might not be a bad idea to reaffirm on the minivan. The risk is no greater than when you took out the loan in the first place. If you default they can come after you for what is owed on the loan, including any deficiency if it is repossessed and sells for something less than the loan balance. The difference, however, is that you will not readily be able to file for bankruptcy relief again, and if your wages are being garnished for a car loan that you reaffirmed you would probably not be able to get any sort of bankruptcy relief to stop that process. On the plus side, you will do some good at repairing your credit; the balance due on the car loan is decreasing and with that the likelihood of a deficiency ever occurring diminishes too.

By reaffirming a debt, you are basically giving up the protection that a bankruptcy filing would automatically be giving you. Therefore, you can see why your lawyer and the court may look like they are trying to talk you out of signing a reaffirmation agreement.

So, back to those four options. The first, (surrender), is easy to understand, you turn over the property that is the collateral on the loan, the debt is discharged in the bankruptcy and you are done with it forever. The second option, reaffirming the debt was discussed above. The third option (redeeming) is almost never done with something like a car loan, there is just too much money involved. But if it involves something like a washing machine you might be able to get Sears, or whoever financed it to acknowledge that it has depreciated, and if it is re-sold they might only get $300 out of it even though you still owe, $1,300. If you agree to pay the $300 they are done, and you can keep the washing machine. That is a redemption agreement, not a reaffirmation agreement, and the Bankruptcy Court does not become involved in those agreements.

If you have a car loan and you do not reaffirm the debt before your discharge is entered in your bankruptcy case, you cannot later reaffirm the debt. So, let's say you are a house painter. You have a truck that you use to do your work. The truck is worth no more than you owe on it, but you need it for work. Work is slow and seasonal. You're pretty sure you can keep up the payments over the summer, but during the winter, maybe not. The Bankruptcy Code only gives you two practical options, surrender the truck or reaffirm the payments or you could offer to redeem the truck by paying the lender what it's worth, but people in Chapter 7 cases never have any money to make such lump sum settlements with their lenders. But maybe a rich relative would help you to do that. So let's forget about the third option and turn to the fourth.

The Code does not recognize the fourth option but I'll bet it is the most common way this is handled. The painter could simply hang onto his truck, sending in his payments monthly as if nothing ever happened, but if things get bad in the winter, he can tell them to come repossess the truck and he would not have to be worried about any deficiency. The big downside to this approach is that if the truck is financed by Ford Motor Credit, or some of the other major lenders they may not wait until winter to find out how this is going to turn out. They may insist on their rights as lenders under the Bankruptcy Code. And if there is not a court approved reaffirmation agreement in place by the time the debtor gets his discharge, an agent for Ford Motor Credit might just show up in your driveway in the middle of the night with a tow truck, even if you are current on your payments.

Ford has the money to hire accountants, economists, MBAs, PhDs and any other talent they need to decide on corporate policy. Ford, like any company, lacks a brain so it doesn't make sense to accuse it of being stupid or acting stupidly. Presumably, the management has done some calculations, evaluated everything thoroughly and come to the conclusion that in the long run they are better off repossessing vehicles from debtors in bankruptcy who are current on their payments, than letting them voluntarily continue making those payments for the remaining life of the loan.

On any individual case, what they do by repossessing a car may appear to be stupid. If they take back a truck that is worth $10,000 retail from someone who is current on his loan and making consistent payments they know first, that the stream of payments will end. They forego collection of the principal and all of the interest that would have been earned on that loan. They also know that they will have costs involved in recovering the car and preparing it for sale. Then there are the sale expenses, and if it is sold into a depressed market, the $10,000 truck might net only a $5,000 recovery for Ford. That does not appear economically wise.

If the car loan was from a local credit union, they might not be quite so eager to realize a $5,000 loss on a performing loan. Why should they? So whether the "playing chicken" strategy will work with your lender or not depends on who the lender is. Your lawyer may be able to help you understand who you need to worry about and who you don't. Or, maybe you could call your bank or credit union and just ask them what they would do if you keep making payments and don't sign a reaffirmation agreement. Remember, whoever you talk to might not understand what you are talking about, or might not have the authority to speak on behalf of the lender, and you could still find your car missing in the middle of the night. These are the risks you have to be willing to assume if you try to keep a car without entering into a reaffirmation agreement. The other thing is that if you do not sign a reaffirmation agreement and the lender does not show up to repossess your car within a month or two after the discharge has been entered, and you remain current on the car, chances are that you have won, and you will be able to complete the payments on the car if you can, or walk away from it if you can no longer afford it. The technical term for this situation is that you have turned a loan into a non-recourse loan. I thought you would want to know that.

UNDERSTANDING LIENS OR ENCUMBRANCES

If you want to borrow money to pay for something, like a car, or a refrigerator, or to start a business, the lender will feel a whole lot more secure lending you the money if they know they can take the car back, or take the refrigerator back, or if they sell off your business equipment and tools if you don't pay them back on time. When you enter into a transaction like this you are voluntarily pledging the car or the refrigerator as collateral. It's like going to a pawn shop and giving them your refrigerator to get a loan, except, in this case, you keep the refrigerator and give them paperwork instead, a security agreement, that says they can come pick up the refrigerator if you don't pay. You may not have bothered to read the ultra-fine print in the Security Agreement when you bought that refrigerator, but basically that's what it said.

If you had taken the refrigerator to a pawn shop to get a loan, the pawn shop would have possession of it and there would be no way you could convince someone else to make a loan to you using the same refrigerator as collateral. But what's to stop you from going to another lender, taking out another loan, and using the same refrigerator as collateral? Well, that would be fraudulent for one thing, but besides that, the answer is the recording system for the paperwork would stop you, that's what. Every state has a system for publicly recording these transactions, and just as importantly, for allowing someone to search the records and find whether you have previously pledged your car, your refrigerator, your business assets or your home, or anything else, as collateral for a loan. When someone has the right to repossess the collateral if you default on the payment, they are said to have a lien on the collateral.

Before making a new loan, a savvy lender would search the public records for possible liens on your property. If they find a lien then they would be more wary about making a loan, if they know they would have to deal with another lender who has already recorded a lien. Generally speaking when it comes to refrigerators, cars and other personal property if there is a lien recorded nobody else would be willing to make a loan. When it comes to your home, or other real property, (real estate), there may be enough equity, that the lender would be willing to make a loan and take their rights to foreclose subject to the rights of the lender who first recorded their interest. That is where home equity loans and second mortgages come from.

The system for recording these liens differs depending on the kind of property involved. The records for cars are kept in one system, the records for other personal property are kept in another set of records, and the system for houses and other real estate is another system. It gets quite complicated, actually, when you get into things like aircraft, and financial instruments, but suffice to say, there is a system for everything. And someone with the motivation to search can figure it out.

If you file a bankruptcy of course your lawyer and the Trustee will both want to figure this out because you may lose that property if you have pledged your property as collateral and you don't live up to your obligations. The Trustee is interested because even if you have pledged it as collateral, if the lender didn't do their paperwork right, and did not properly "perfect:" their lien, it may turn out that the Trustee can "avoid" that lien, and step into the creditor's shoes and the Trustee, rather than the Creditor can be the one repossessing the property from you. This is very important, because even though you normally have an exemption that would protect your interest in your car, refrigerator, or home, when you signed the paperwork you waived that exemption. After all, it wouldn't make much sense, would it, if you borrowed the money to finance a car purchase, didn't pay, and then when the lender came to pick up the car, you claimed that the car was exempt? That wouldn't work at all, these lenders make sure you waive your exemption rights. Therefore, if the Trustee can avoid the lender's lien and step into its shoes, the Trustee could repossess the property. Fortunately for everybody, except the trustee, financial institutions that make these loans know what they're doing and they usually get it right, which means that the Trustee seldom gets the opportunity to avoid the lien and recover the collateral.

These systems of recording liens are used for things other than consensual liens among consenting adults. They are used for recording non-consensual liens, judgment liens and that kind of thing as well.

So, if, for example, you failed to pay your taxes for a year or two, the IRS may file its notice in these public records indicating it has put a lien on your property even without your consent. Or if you fail to pay a credit card, or two, and they file suit and get a judgment for the amounts owed, they would probably file a notice of the judgment, and that would attach to your property as a lien.

People often fear that someone will put a lien on their property without their consent. Nobody can do that legally without due process. The IRS has its process, and for everything else it means there will have to be an arbitration or court proceeding resulting in a judgment that can be recorded. Collection agents who threaten to put a lien on property are jumping a few steps ahead; they cannot do so before getting a judgment. But, they have become fairly good at getting judgments so that is not a completely empty threat.

AVOIDING LIENS ON PROPERTY

So, now that you know what a lien is, you can easily understand what avoiding a lien might mean. Just like it sounds, it's just like what happens when that cute cheerleader sees you coming down the hall in your middle school nightmare, and she avoids you, acting as if you don't matter at all, in fact as if you don't even exist.

The Bankruptcy Code picked up on that concept and put it into the law. In certain circumstances, a perfectly legal and valid lien can be avoided. It doesn't cease to exist, the paperwork is all still there, but just like that wilting middle school boy, the world gets the message that it's OK to treat it as if it does not exist. Most things in life have to be avoided *before* they happen. You can avoid spilling a soft drink in your lap if you are careful, but in the real world, you cannot avoid a soft drink in your lap *after* the drink is spilled. But in the magical world of bankruptcy, you can avoid a lien, after the lien has attached to property.

But, this doesn't happen very often, in the bankruptcy world at least, because there are some important words that limit when it can happen.

The law begins by grandly proclaiming: "Notwithstanding any waiver of exemptions..."

And anytime a law begins with a word like "Notwithstanding", you know it's about to erase a whole bunch of things. So the word notwithstanding, followed by "any waiver of exemptions" means, basically; forget about the fact that you may have signed a waiver of your rights to exempt property. It is then followed by the phrase; "the debtor may avoid the fixing of a lien on an interest of the debtor". It takes someone like my old contracts law professor to come up with language like that, when what they were really trying to say was: You can avoid a lien on your property even if you waived your exemptions. When? If it "impairs an exemption."

OK, so, so far, I understand that a debtor can avoid a lien on their property if that property would otherwise be exempt, even if they waived their exemptions. That's pretty awesome! Remember just a few paragraphs back I was saying that if you didn't waive your exemptions the system would not work, lenders would not make loans if they could not get their collateral back. Once again, this is the power of the Bankruptcy Code, to alter the relations between borrowers and lenders in very powerful way.

But, we're not done yet. They start out with this broad language and then they take most of it back. This only applies if the lien is a judicial lien (with some exceptions to that even), meaning a judgment that has been recorded; or, if it is a nonpossessory, nonpurchase-money security interest in household goods, etcetera. So back to my refrigerator example, if you financed the purchase of that refrigerator they gave you the purchase-money and this concept only applies to nonpurchase-money. So the lien of *The Great Indoors* who sold you the refrigerator would stick through the bankruptcy case. On the other hand, if you went to *ABC Home Finance Company*, and took out an emergency loan, and you used your refrigerator and some other household goods that you already owned as collateral for that loan, their lien could be avoided.

Since most car loans involve the purchase-money that was used to pay for the car, and for other reasons, this kind of lien avoidance does not generally come up for car loans.

On the other hand, this tool of the Bankruptcy Code is very important if you own your own home, and you have been sued, and you intend to keep your house. In that situation, even if you don't have any equity in your house you are probably keeping it because you expect you will some day. Or maybe you would had some equity in your house, then you got sued, and now between the amount of your mortgage and the amount of your judgment lien, it looks like you don't have any equity. In these situations, you can use this tool to avoid the judgment lien and free up that equity. The actual process for avoiding the lien is not particularly complicated, but it does involve a procedure to get a ruling from the Bankruptcy Judge. If you think you are in this situation you should discuss it with your lawyer and see whether you qualify and whether your lawyer can help you with this. If you are doing this on your own, good luck. The Court is not going to guide you through this.

If you have really been paying attention you would understand that a lien for a second mortgage or a home equity loan cannot be avoided in a bankruptcy case even if it is a non-possessory, nonpurchase-money security interest, because it is not an interest in the household goods and related items described by the statute.

So, in review, if a creditor got a judgment against you and recorded a lien on your house and you want to make that lien go away, or if you pledged your exempt household goods as collateral on a loan and you want to keep that property, it would be a good idea to discuss avoiding these liens with your lawyer and see whether you can make them go away. It is not always possible for all kinds of reasons. But the important thing to remember is that in just the right circumstances dealing with these liens during the bankruptcy can free you up from a problem you have, that you might not have even known you have.

SHORT SALES

"What happens to my home?" That is the first thing that most homeowners want to know about when they consider bankruptcy. Or maybe they are in way too deep on a home mortgage and just want to find a way to get out and move on with life. What you do with your house is up to you to decide. You really can do whatever you want, if you can live with the consequences.

If you like your home and you want to stay in it and you think you can afford to keep making the mortgage payments there is a strong probability you will be able to keep it. And, if you don't like your house, or you need to move, or you love your house but can't handle the house payments, then there is a way to deal with that too.

This book is focused on using bankruptcy as a remedy for financial problems. But, let's say that you have one huge financial problem and a few minor ones. If you could deal with the big one, the fact that you owe way more on your house than you can sell it for, then the little problems would all be manageable. What if you could get rid of your house and not owe anything more for it? Would that allow you to get your life back under control without going through a bankruptcy process?

Be realistic, prepare a budget. Look at how much you are paying now for your home mortgage, insurance, groceries and everything else compared with what you are bringing in. If you could eliminate the home mortgage payment that would be a change, but you probably have to pay for housing wherever you go, so you would have to add an estimated expense for rent even if you are willing to let the house go. After you add back in a projected rent expense how much is left to pay for everything else? If there is enough then you could probably avoid a bankruptcy filing just by getting rid of the house.

You might want to take a look at the flip side, while you are at it. If you could eliminate all or most of your other debts, would you then be able to afford your house payment and keep your house. You may be able to choose either course.

Let's say you realized that even if you got rid of the house payment and substituted in a rent payment there will still not be enough money to deal with all the remaining debt. You will probably file for bankruptcy and if you do, you do not need to be particularly concerned with selling your house. You may want to just stay in it either paying the house payments and hoping for better times or letting them lapse, and waiting to be foreclosed.

Now let's say you prepared a budget and realized that your financial problems all revolve around a mortgage expense that is too high and you are ready to do something about it. You are ready to move on. If you were not "under water"; that is owing more on your home than it is worth, you would simply call up a realtor when you are ready to sell, get the house listed, and get it sold. But if you are "under water" you have to be more careful in how you do this.

You may want to contract a broker who specializes in short-sales. I suspect this is a growing specialty. A typical contract with a realtor provides that if they can find a buyer at the price you specify who is willing and capable of closing the sale, they you owe them a sales commission even if the sale does not close. If the sale price of the house is close to the amount owed, you could be in the awkward position of having to show up with cash at the closing to close the sale and to assure that the realtor gets paid. And if you don't have the cash, they could sue you for it if you decided not to close. But this rarely happens, Realtors survive on their reputations and anyone who got a reputation for suing their customers would quickly find that they didn't get very many new listings. So, despite the listing contract's provisions the person you hired to assist in the sale of your home will probably try to make a deal happen, even if the value of the house is not enough to pay off the mortgage or mortgages.

The name of the game is compromise. The first thing to go is any money you hoped to get out of the sale. The next thing is to convince the lender that you are not particularly wealthy, that you can't afford to make the house payments, so they are not likely to get much of anything out of you if they foreclose on the property and sell it at market value and then sue you for the balance of the loan. If they realize that their only hope on this loan is to get as much as they can out of your home as quickly as possible, then you have a good shot at convincing them to do a short sale. You should not expect the realtor to give up part of their fee, typically that does not happen even in a short sale.

A good way to think about these situations is that these are called short sales because someone is coming up short on the amount they expected to get. The term probably comes from the financial community where a short sale involves selling something you don't already own. In a sense that's true for a short sale of a home. At the time of the sale you owe more on it than it's worth yet you are giving the buyer a Warranty Deed and the warranty they get, is that they will own the home free and clear of any liens that are on it. In a normal sale, the liens are all paid off by the closing agent from the sale proceeds and you get what's left. In a short sale, everyone knows the sale proceeds will be insufficient to pay off those liens.

Part of what makes our real estate market work so efficiently, is that it is not based on trust at all. Nobody trusts anybody. Suppose you are desperate to sell your house, you find someone willing to buy it and you promise them that once they have paid, they will own it free and clear of any liens that there are already on the house. You promise to give them a Warranty Deed to the property at closing. But, frankly, what good is a warranty from you? You're moving, who knows where. And if you are wrong about that promise what are the buyers supposed to do, track you down, sue you and get their money back? That just wouldn't work. So we have Title Insurance. You not only give the buyer your warranty, but you tell them you will back it up with insurance. If you're working with a realtor they arrange all that, but one of the line items you will see on a settlement statement is a fee you are paying the title company to provide the buyer with a policy of title insurance. That way if you were wrong that you could deliver title free and clear of all liens, the buyer doesn't need to track you down at all, they just make an insurance claim. Obviously the Title Insurance companies would not stay in business very long if they had to pay out very often. So they make sure you can deliver title free and clear of liens. And since the title companies often handle the closing, they know that if they are going to insure title, they can make sure you can actually deliver good title.

But, how can you do that, if you owe more than the property is worth and you don't have the money to cover the difference? You get an agreement with the lender or lenders to accept a short payoff in return for which they agree to release their lien on the property.

There's short and there's short though. The lender could agree to release the lien on the condition that you give them a lien on another piece of property, but that will never happen. Or they could agree to release the lien if you agree to pay the difference. Or they could simply forgive the balance of the debt.

Most of the time when people are talking about a short sale, they are talking about a situation where the lender agrees to accept a payment of a specified amount from the closing proceeds in exchange for a release of its lien on the property and forgiveness of the remaining debt. If you are dealing with a realtor, or a lender, in a short-sale transaction it is pretty important to have a clear understanding with the lender whether they are releasing just their lien on the property or whether they are releasing that and releasing you from the remaining obligation.

If there is a first and a second on the property you need to make sure you have an agreement with both of them and that everyone understands what they will get from the deal when it closes.

But, even if you get a complete release from all lien holders, that does not prevent them from sending you a form 1099 for the amount of the debt that they have forgiven. That could create an unforeseen tax liability. But, as I explain elsewhere, that usually is something that can be avoided. You will not have to pay taxes on the forgiven debt if you can convince the IRS that you are insolvent.

What I don't understand is people who have filed for relief in a bankruptcy case who contact me because they are on the verge of closing on a short sale of their house. Why? What do they care? I understand that there may be some small benefit in terms of rebuilding a credit rating by having just a bankruptcy on the record instead of a bankruptcy followed by a foreclosure, but seriously, does it really make any difference? In many cases people could probably hang out in their homes for months or years without making payments after a bankruptcy filing, why are they so eager to get them sold. Maybe it's the responsible thing to do. A lot of times the only person who cares is the real estate agent who hopes to earn a commission on a sale. Perhaps they have been trying for months to sell the property without success. Their client files for bankruptcy and then suddenly there is an offer to purchase the property. The lender is easily convinced that accepting a payoff at whatever amount the market dictates will be their best option. But for the debtors the benefits of doing a short sale of property after a bankruptcy filing are harder to find. As soon as the property is sold they will have to move and start paying rent somewhere else.

 But there are some benefits to getting rid of real estate. What if, long after you abandoned it, a squatter came in and turned it into a meth lab, and after destroying the property, the government authorities tracked you down to pay for the clean-up costs? Or, if the property is part of a Homeowner's Association, in most places the Association can continue to assess dues to the homeowner after a bankruptcy for so long as the title to the property remains in their name. If a lender takes years to foreclose, the HOA could insist on payment of its post-bankruptcy dues and the homeowner has no defense.

So to review, if you want or need to sell your house and you owe more than you can get out of it, you will have to arrange a short sale. You cannot assume you will be able to get cooperation. There are probably thousands of very wonderful people who work for the companies that hold and service mortgage debt. Some are quite pleasant to deal with. But the companies themselves have no real financial incentive to try to keep you happy or to make your experience more pleasant. These companies exist to make sure that the people who are entitled to collect the debt get their money. And one of the problems that has become very obvious is that there is often literally nobody who has authority to negotiate directly with you to adjust payment terms. That all has to do with the way these home loans have been turned into securities and sold. In fact, it is a bit of a wonder that there is any system at all for negotiating short sales. But fortunately, there is.

For these companies it comes down to this: Are they better off letting you sell the house and getting what its currently worth out of it or not? If they decide they will not be better off, they may think that you will continue to make payments, but maybe you won't. Then they would have to foreclose. They would eventually get the house back and have to sell it. By the time they sell it will the market be better or worse. Will they have to recognize a loss on their books right away or can they delay that?

I don't know what percentage of attempted short-sales are successful. One Massachusetts Realtor authoritatively stated on-line that less than 30% of the transactions are successful. Others put the figure at 5% or 10%. But any national statistic on this is meaningless. Whether you can successfully sell your house short depends on who your lender is, what the local market conditions are, the condition of your property, your overall financial condition, and other factors. If you can work with a realtor who is experienced at doing these, you will know right away whether you will be successful. If the realtor is willing to spend their time, effort and marketing budget to find a buyer, knowing that you owe more than the local market will bring, chances are they believe you will be able to get the lender to agree to the terms of the sale as well.

BANKRUPTCY JARGON

It is helpful to know the language anywhere you travel, and bankruptcy land is no exception. The language used in bankruptcy land is a dialect of the English language. It uses English as a base and takes off from there. If you ever listened to cricket scores, which you can do anytime you want on the BBC, you might realize as I have, that you can understand every word but still understand nothing of what they have said. It sounds something like this: "Pakistan leads Sri Lanka in the best-of cup, 71 to 22 with 5 overs, after three days of play, bowling to an empty wicket." And I have no idea what they are talking about. Likewise you can understand all the words but not understand the Bankruptcy Code. Take the following paragraph for example. This is an actual paragraph from the bankruptcy code found at 11 U.S.C. § 547(i):

> If the trustee avoids under subsection (b) a transfer made between 90 days and 1 year before the date of the filing of the petition, by the debtor to an entity that is not an insider for the benefit of a creditor that is an insider, such transfer shall be considered to be avoided under this section only with respect to the creditor that is an insider.

I'll bet you understand the conventional meaning of every word in that paragraph, but still have no idea what it is saying. Right?

Like learning any language it takes time and practice to get fluent. We are not going there. This is going to be the equivalent of having a phrase book so that you can do the equivalent of ordering a beer, and then asking the location of the toilet.

As to the paragraph above, it's not worth going into it too deeply; it just has to do with who the trustee can recover from if the trustee is trying to claw-back property that was transferred within the year before the bankruptcy case was filed.

It is not necessary to learn to read this language, but knowing a few phrases and how they are used, just like knowing how to ask where the toilet is in a country speaking a foreign language, can be quite useful. The following terms are the useful ones to know.

DISCHARGE AND DISMISS

A Debtor in a bankruptcy case files in order to get a Discharge of their debts. That "Discharge" is what the Court sends out to notify creditors that the debts involved in the bankruptcy have been discharged. A normal person would say that the debts were cancelled, voided, eliminated or bankrupted, but none of these synonyms is exactly correct, the entry of a discharge releases the debtor from legal liability on all the debts included in the discharge to the extent the law allows.

That is quite different from having a court enter an order of Dismissal. What that means is that the court has thrown out the case. When a case is dismissed there is no Discharge. Creditors are free to resume their efforts to collect debt. But, if a debtor had a previous case dismissed and did not receive a discharge, the requirements in the code that require waiting a period of years before re-filing a case do not apply and the debtor can re-file at any time.

Likewise, a denial or revocation of a discharge is not a good thing for a debtor. It means on the one hand that the court has found a reason to prevent a debtor from getting a discharge, and on the other hand it means that that the court has found reason to take back a discharge after already granting one. Both are possible, but both are rare.

EXCEPTIONS AND EXEMPTIONS

The two words sound alike and therefore tend to get mixed up. Understanding them is important. The Bankruptcy Code is full of exceptions. You will get discharged from most debt except those things listed in a particular place in the Code. A creditor can seek an exception to discharge if they think they can prove to a judge that their claim qualifies as one of the exceptions.

Exemptions are something completely different. Property that is exempt is property that the trustee cannot take away from you. And, unfortunately there is an exception to what I just said. For example, in a state where an exemption of $5,000 is allowed for your equity in a car, and you own a car worth $10,000 that has been paid off, the Trustee could, in fact, sell your car, but he would have to give you back $5,000 of the money received from that sale. So, technically I was not correct when I said the Trustee could not take your car away from you because you have a valid exemption claimed. Ordinarily the Trustee would find some way to get the equity value out of the car without forcing the sale if there is a reasonable way.

Another way to understand this is that almost everything becomes property of the bankruptcy estate when a case is filed. The trustee must then determine whether there is any property that is free of encumbrances (see below) and not claimed as exempt, which might be worth liquidating to provide a benefit to creditors.

DEBTOR AND CREDITOR

The persons who file for bankruptcy relief are called the debtors. If it's just one person he or she is "the debtor." There are still some attorneys around who refer to this person as "the bankrupt." If you run into such an attorney you will notice that he has either white or gray hair, if any hair is left. That was the term that was used until the Bankruptcy Code was revamped in 1986. If someone is still using that term you can be pretty sure that they have not kept up on the bankruptcy law. It is handy to know that sometimes.

A **creditor** is the person or more commonly the "entity" who is owed money by the debtor. Presidential candidates may be adamant about the fact that corporations are persons, or corporations are not persons. It really does simplify things to use fewer words sometimes and I'm somewhat surprised that Congress can bring itself to do that. In the paragraph quoted from the Code it used the phrase "*to an entity*," it could have instead said, "*to a person or persons, Corporation, Limited Liability Company, Limited Liability Partnership, Trust, Estate or Governmental unit*." At least that's what I thought was included in the term entity.

Some terms are defined by the Code and the Code's definition of the term "entity" does not include everything I mentioned. It leaves out Corporation, Limited Liability Company etc. How can that be? Let's look at the definition of the term "person." You would think that of all the words in the English language if the Bankruptcy Code is going to limit itself to defining only 55 of them it would skip the word "person" and assume that we all know what a person is. But it is precisely because we don't all know what a person is that the term is defined. In bankruptcy land, a "person" includes individual, partnership and corporation, but does not include a governmental unit. Another of the 55 words the Code bothers to define is "United States." I don't think I need to cover that one.

CLAIM

A claim happens to be another of the terms that is defined in the Bankruptcy Code. The reason it is defined is that it is intended to include just about anything, and the people who wrote the Code expressed that in a legalistic definition. Rather than using two paragraphs of words to describe what a claim is, it would be helpful to just think that anyone who is owed money, or thinks they are owed money or was wronged and could seek money damages has a claim. Whether the claim is valid or not can be and sometimes is disputed.

ENCUMBRANCE AND EQUITY

Encumbrance is not one of those words that most people, other than bankruptcy lawyers, use in everyday conversation. Understanding what an encumbrance is is important to understanding how this system works. The Bankruptcy Code doesn't bother to define this term though. And, rather than turning to a dictionary for a formal definition, I won't try to define it, I'll just describe it.

Property can become encumbered either voluntarily or involuntarily. I frequently hear from people who are worried about someone putting a lien on their house without their consent. It does happen but it's not that common. Most liens are given with consent.

It works like this: You go to buy a house and you just don't happen to have enough cash to pay for the house on the day of closing. For you and the rest of the 99% this is always how it works. So you need to finance part of the purchase price. You may pay a small down payment and finance the balance of the purchase price and closing costs by taking out a mortgage. That mortgage arrangement consists of two principal documents: a Promissory Note and a Mortgage or Deed of Trust. The idea is that the promissory note specifies the payment plan, and the mortgage specifies what happens if you don't pay according to plan. The lender makes sure that the mortgage is filed with the appropriate county clerk and recorder so that anyone who is curious enough to investigate can find out that you have pledged your house as collateral for repayment of the loan you took out to purchase it. It works basically the same way with a car loan. Except with car loans the lender makes sure anyone investigating can find that they have "first dibs" on the car if payments aren't made according to plan. By the way, "first dibs" is not a legal term, it's something I picked up on the playground at elementary school, but the concept is the same.

In both of the examples above, the lender has "encumbered" the property by "perfecting their security interest." Both lenders have a "lien" on the property, and in both cases it was done consensually, or with the borrower's consent.

Moving to the next concept, **Equity,** is calculated by taking the value of property and subtracting the encumbrances. A lot of people understand this concept, but not very many people think about their property in this way. The bankruptcy process is very focused on the equity in any asset, not its value so much. For example if a debtor owns a home that is worth $350,000 and owes a mortgage on it of $320,000, that person has $30,000 of equity. The question then, in bankruptcy is what happens to that $30,000 of equity. Fortunately, for most people, in most states, that amount of equity would be exempt, and the trustee would not even consider selling the house.

I described consensual liens above, that is liens given with consent, but there are other types of encumbrances as well. Say you happened to be sued by a credit card company and they get a judgment against you. That judgment typically would get recorded in the public records in the same place that the mortgage is recorded, so that when you go to sell or refinance the house the new buyer or lender wants to make sure that it is paid off so that they can get clear title to the property. They encumber the property by putting a judgment lien on it. The bankruptcy process can sometimes remove these liens, and if you think there may be some such liens on your property it is a good idea to talk to your lawyer about this. The IRS could also encumber your property by recording a lien for unpaid taxes.

By understanding the concept of encumbrances and equity you can more easily see what is likely to happen in your bankruptcy case. The Trustee is generally only interested in the property in which you have some equity, regardless of the value of your property. The secured creditors are not really interested in your bankruptcy case, they just want to know whether you are going to keep paying them or you are going to give them back the property you pledged as collateral. This is done by filing a document in the case known as a Statement of Intentions. You will need to discuss these concepts with your attorney and decide what you intend to do. But don't worry, like any intention, it can change and you are not locked in to what you file with the court forever.

FREQUENTLY ASKED QUESTIONS

Q: Will a bankruptcy stop a garnishment?
A: Yes.

Q: Will a bankruptcy stop a foreclosure?
A: It will stop it temporarily at least?

Q: I am being sued, and I don't have any defense, do I need to file before a judgment is entered against me?
A: For a typical collection case you do not need to file before a judgment is entered, but
There may be reasons why you would want to do so, such as preventing a court from entering findings of fact that could be damaging, or preventing a lien from being recorded on real estate that you own.

Q: How long does a bankruptcy take?
A: That depends on what you are asking about. A filing can be done electronically, and the Order for relief goes into effect instantly. Typically it takes a little over 3 months to get a discharge and have the case closed. If assets are being liquidated and distributed it may take years before the case is closed. And, a Chapter 13 case will take at least 3 years and most likely 5 years to complete.

Q: How much does a bankruptcy cost?
A: See the section in the book on that topic.

Q: Can I keep some credit cards?
A: If you have a zero balance owed on a card, that card issuer is not listed as a creditor and does not automati-

cally receive notice from the court. But, major creditors become aware of bankruptcy filings and may cancel a card even if nothing is owed.

Q: Can I keep my bank account?
A: You can keep a bank account. Frequently a Credit Union will expel you as a member if they have to take a loss because of a bankruptcy. Money in the account is considered property of the bankruptcy estate, subject to applicable exemptions, and may need to be turned over to the trustee.

Q: Do I need to change where I do my banking?
A: You do not need to change where you bank, but some banks may freeze an account with a large balance for the benefit of the trustee, or a bank may exercise its right of setoff, paying itself for a debt owed to the bank, shortly before the bankruptcy case is filed.

Q: How will this affect my credit score?
A: Generally it is safe to assume that a bankruptcy will lower your credit score, probably significantly, especially if you are current on your bills when you file, which is not that unusual. In some cases the score improves because of the elimination of debt.

Q: If the Trustee is going to take my (fill in the blank) anyway, can I transfer it to my brother to keep that from happening?
A: No.

Q: Do I qualify for bankruptcy?

A: Pretty much all people qualify for bankruptcy, but, if you have previously filed for Chapter 7 bankruptcy within the past 8 years and received a discharge you will not be eligible for a discharge. Unsecured debts in excess of $360,475 (as adjusted from time to time) will keep you from qualifying for a Chapter 13 Bankruptcy. There are other limitations as well. More important considerations are whether or not filing for bankruptcy is a good idea and timing the filing to get maximum advantage.

Q: Will I be able to keep my gun/car/house/spouse?

A: See the section of this book on what you get to keep. For the gun, car and house, whether you get to keep them depends generally on how much they are worth, the amount of your equity in them, and the exemption laws where you reside. For the Spouse, a bankruptcy might help end arguments over money, but beyond that, the bankruptcy law is not relevant. You are pretty much on your own on figuring that one out.

ABOUT THE AUTHOR

I skipped the class in law school called Debtor/Creditor. That's the one where they taught about Bankruptcy Law. At the time I couldn't think of anything that sounded more boring than that. I did not grow up dreaming that one day I would become a bankruptcy lawyer. I wonder if anyone ever did. How I became a bankruptcy lawyer was really a process of elimination as much as anything else. Although I enjoy what I do, being a bankruptcy lawyer is a bit toxic for conversation. You start with the natural skepticism everybody shares about lawyers and layer on to that this specialty where you are dealing with people who are broke   Sometimes people say something like, "I'm, sorry", as if I just announced I have cancer, but lately I've seen eyebrows raise, and the most common response is, well, your business must be thriving

One of my colleagues described the business of being a bankruptcy trustee as being a financial undertaker of the financial world. That's a pretty good description. I have been burying the corpses of failed financial enterprises and individual's dreams for over 24 years.

Coming out of law school in New Hampshire, I was fired up to do public policy work on energy policy. But Jimmy Carter did not get re-elected and since then the United States has been unable to develop any kind of coherent energy policy at a state or federal level. I worked for a few years trying to do energy policy before it became clear to me that whatever I had gone to law school to achieve, that was not it.

I started my own private practice and learned that I was not cut out for doing criminal representation, nor family law. Bankruptcy seemed to be a good fit, and clients seemed to actually appreciate what I could do for them. A friend of mine got me set up as a Bankruptcy Trustee, back when the pay was really low, and there was not a lot of interest doing it, I have persisted, and prospered.

I have handled many thousands of bankruptcy cases as a trustee, and hundreds of cases as counsel for individuals. After hearing the questions, repeating the answers hundreds of times I think I have as good a feel as anyone about the things that matter to people when they are contemplating bankruptcy or going through the process. Many books on the topic contain material that some scholar or editor for some reason thought was important. There are seminars for bankruptcy attorneys that have topics on subjects I've never even heard about. A bankruptcy attorney who works for a bank would have a completely different point of view than mine and would be knowledgeable about things I don't know about.

By working both sides of the fence, representing debtors and collecting from debtors I have developed a unique perspective. If you don't know which side of the fence you will be on, it's much harder to get rigid in your beliefs about what is fair or not in one situation or another.

I've also seen how harsh the dialogue and the commentary about anything has become on the internet. I've seen completely wrong or misleading posts about some bankruptcy topics. And, I've seen cynical posts where distrust of lawyers causes people to do stupid things. Yes, I'm a lawyer, and yes, I do think lawyers provide a valuable service, that does not make me so blind or so biased that I would steer you into doing something that is not good. Remember, I am not going to profit if you decide to file bankruptcy. It makes no financial difference to me. I just think I have learned a few things, and as the boy said at the end of the movie, *The Sixth Sense*, "I am ready to communicate now." It's my way of giving back for a very interesting, rewarding career.

www.ingramcontent.com/pod-product-compliance
Lightning Source LLC
Chambersburg PA
CBHW051215170526
45166CB00005B/1910